# POLITICAL PHILOSOPHY NOW

*Chief Editor of the Series:*
Howard Williams, Aberystwyth University, Wales

*Associate Editors:*
Wolfgang Kersting, University of Kiel, Germany
Steven B. Smith, Yale University, USA
Peter Nicholson, University of York, England
Renato Cristi, Wilfrid Laurier University, Waterloo, Canada

**Political Philosophy Now** is a series which deals with authors, topics and periods in political philosophy from the perspective of their relevance to current debates. The series presents a spread of subjects and points of view from various traditions, which include European and New World debates in political philosophy.

POLITICAL PHILOSOPHY NOW

# Deleuze and Guattari: Aesthetics and Politics

Robert Porter

UNIVERSITY OF WALES PRESS • CARDIFF • 2009

*www.uwp.co.uk*

*British Library Cataloguing-in-Publication Data*
A catalogue record for this book is available from the British Library.

ISBN 978-0-7083-2159-1
e-ISBN 978-0-7083-2231-4

The right of Robert Porter to be identified as author of this work has been asserted by him in accordance with sections 77, 78 and 79 of the Copyright, Designs and Patents Act 1988.

Printed in Great Britain by CPI Antony Rowe, Chippenham, Wiltshire

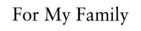

For My Family

# Contents

# Acknowledgements

Thanks to colleagues and friends in the School of Media, Film and Journalism at the University of Ulster for enlivening my thought and sharing the odd joke or two along the way. As director of the Media Studies Research Institute at the University of Ulster, Máire Messenger-Davies provided financial support which gave me more autonomy and space to think and write. I am very grateful for help from graduate students and colleagues in sharing some of my teaching responsibilities during the writing of the book; I would particularly like to give my thanks to Ciara Chambers and Phil Ramsey. I am also grateful to those undergraduate students in my Aesthetics and Politics class who critically engaged with much of the material set out in this book and, in so doing, helped me clarify my own thinking.

For many a fascinating conversation about the relation between aesthetics and politics, for allowing me to appropriate his ideas and his work as an artist, for reading and commenting on parts of the manuscript as it was developing, I am grateful to Daniel Jewesbury. Deepest thanks also go to my friend and long-time intellectual comrade Iain Mackenzie for reading significant chunks of the manuscript and making my 'encounter' with Deleuze and Guattari more vital than it would otherwise have been. Last, but by no means least, I am indebted to Sarah Lewis and Dafydd Jones at the University of Wales Press for their patience, responsiveness and support of this project.

Closer to home, and most importantly, I want to give my most heartfelt thanks to my remarkable family; particularly my wife Kerry-Ann and daughters Jessica and Anna. Jessica and Anna are the comic-philosopher-architects in our house, humorously constructing a world that is in constant need of ever-new concepts or ideas, ideas which provoke us all to renew our thinking. Kerry-Ann is a constant source of love, commitment and support.

This book is dedicated to my family.

# Introduction

This short book is intended to perform a rather specific two-fold function, namely (a) to give a feel for some of Gilles Deleuze and Félix Guattari's writings on the arts and (b) to extrapolate from these writings the idea that thinking the political, that political theory if you like, can have aesthetic form.[1] Or, put another way; that the arts as such can be thought to be forms of political theory. So how, then, can Deleuze and Guattari's writings be mobilized in order to render concrete the idea that the arts can be thought to be forms of political theory? The core guiding intuition here is this: that the arts always-already are forms of political theory to the degree that they actively exercize their capacity – we could also call this their autonomy – to think the political and, in so doing, shift the meanings we may subsequently attach to the 'political'. This intuition is implicitly and explicitly at play in Deleuze and Guattari's writings on the arts, and we can begin to see this when considering their engagements with language and literature, painting and architecture.[2]

In chapter one, we will engage Deleuze and Guattari's writings on language and literature, in particular their philosophy of language and linguistics as outlined in *A Thousand Plateaus* and their treatment of the literature of Franz Kafka in *Kafka*.[3] In the first part of the chapter, we shall see emerge two important intuitions that give shape to a Deleuze-Guattarian analysis of language. First, they insist on affirming the power, vitality or capacity – the autonomy – of language to intervene directly in the social and political field. Second, there is a critical dismantling of the notion that language somehow finds its primary function in representation, where 'representation' means the communication or exchange of information. As will be seen, Deleuze and Guattari's philosophy of language implies an encounter with a series of concepts or conceptual terms – for instance, 'indirect discourse', the 'collective assemblage of enunciation', 'order-word' or 'slogan' – that all seek to foreground the capacity and power of words to shape and order things in the social-political world. Put simply, Deleuze and Guattari force us to confront the idea that there is always a becoming-political in the things we name 'language and literature' precisely because naming, or language-use, implies a shaping or ordering of the 'political' as such, rather than its re-presentation.

So, if language has a capacity and power to intervene directly in the political, if it can shape the meaning we attach to the 'political' as such, then this obviously implies that our very concept of the political, the political concepts we use in investing meaning or significance in our world, assume a form that is mediated through language-use. As we shall see, particularly in the second and third parts of chapter one, this intuition very much informs the way Deleuze and Guattari engage a body of 'literature' such as Kafka's. In *Kafka*, Deleuze and Guattari are expressly concerned to emphasize the political thinking that is expressed in and through his writing. Two points are worth anticipating here. First, that Kafka's concept of the political is immediately connected to a form of writing that is 'comic' or 'humorous' where, for example, political authority is subject to a comic or humorous exaggeration and critique; a 'becoming-molecular' as Deleuze and Guattari would say.[4] Second, we shall see that political concepts such as 'Law' become subject to a critique in a Kafka novel like *The Trial* to the extent that they are caught up in a movement that is defamiliarizing or, in Deleuze-Guattarian terms, 'deterritorializing'. It is crucial to emphasize that Deleuze and Guattari would consider Kafka's writing as something that embodies and autonomously enacts this movement; a deterritorialization of the world that 'is itself political' as they put it. Put simply, Kafka's writing or use of language does not simply mediate the political by commenting or making representations about how, for example, the law works or ought to work; it directly and immediately thinks the political through the movements it charts, the concepts it creates and, consequently, the deterritorializations it brings about.[5]

In chapter two we move onto Deleuze and Guattari's writings on painting, witnessing this continued and sustained emphasis on the deterritorializing power of the arts. As we shall see, particularly in the second part of the chapter, the Deleuze and Guattari of *A Thousand Plateaus* are specifically interested in the way that painting can function to deterritorialize what they call the 'face', and in the way this deterritorialization of the face implies or thinks a particular concept of ethics and politics. It is important to point out that I preface Deleuze and Guattari's writings here by spending some time in the first part of the chapter discussing the concept of the 'face' found in the work of Emmanuel Levinas. Why, then, this initial focus on Levinas when my express concern is with Deleuze and Guattari? Well, and as will be seen, the primary function or impetus behind the intended juxtaposition of Levinasian and Deleuze-Guattarian images of the face is the creation of a montage, the effect of which will be to bring into focus the key point that there is an ethics as well as a politics implicit in Deleuze and Guattari's critical engagement with painting. Therefore, and in spite of key and fundamental differences, we shall see emerge a kind of formal connection between Levinas and Deleuze-Guattari to the extent that they share a concern to ethico-politically disrupt a rather pernicious politics of the gaze, or a 'politics of recognition', which functions to drown difference in, what Deleuze and Guattari call in rather Levinasian terms, 'waves of sameness'.[6]

So how, then, is a deterritorialization of the face actualized in the specific medium of painting? How does painting deterritorialize and precipitate what Deleuze and Guattari would call the 'minoritarian becomings' that counter any 'politics of recognition' that drowns difference in 'waves of sameness'? In the third and final part of the chapter we will look to Deleuze's specific engagement with Francis Bacon's work; that is, how Bacon's painting effects 'the deterritorialization of faces' and actualizes minoritarian becomings which are at once ethical and political. Key here, we will see, is Baconian portraiture and the singularly evocative notion of, what Deleuze and Guattari would call, 'becoming-animal' that emerges from Bacon's portraits and heads. And it will become crucial to be sensitive to how Bacon's painterly ability to bring to life a 'becoming-animal' implies or thinks an ethics and a politics of the *body as meat*.[7] The stress here should be on how a medium such as painting is poorly understood for as long as we rest content with the idea that it trades in images that simply re-present, communicate or mediate things; in this case, the reality of minoritarian becoming. Bacon's painting, Deleuze insists, is always-already caught up in a form of minoritarian becoming; it is immediately caught up in this very deterritorializing movement to the extent that it sets things in motion through the 'violence' of certain painterly techniques – for example, the 'free manual marks' actualized in and through brushing, rubbing, scratching, throwing paint ...[8]

Arts such as painting and literature do not just mediate the real through commentary or representation; *they are real* to the degree that they participate in, or precipitate, a certain movement in the order of things. As we shall see, this idea of movement and change can be connected to what Deleuze and Guattari would call 'fabulation', where 'fabulation' is a kind of active political philosophy, where its political function is, as they put it, to call forth a 'new earth' or a 'new people'; that is, to create new forms of political subjectivity. Indeed, one of my main concerns in the third and final chapter is to essay the connection between this very notion of 'fabulation' and Deleuze and Guattari's writings on architecture or, more broadly put, built form.[9] So if architecture is an art or form capable of fabulation, then this is because it can create 'blocs of sensation'[10] or can 'fold forces'[11] in order to bring about a shift in our sensibilities regarding the social and political world we inhabit.

Importantly, we shall see that Deleuze and Guattari insist that the fabulating and deterritorializing function they generally attribute to the art-work, and to particular forms such as architecture, should be approached in terms of what they call a 'utopianism' of the 'now-here', and that there is nothing elusive, dramatically heroic or other-worldly about the creation of a new form of political subjectivity. As I will argue at the end of chapter three, the assumption of a new form of political subjectivity can be as small (and as big) as a shift in subjective attitude and thinking, a different take on the social and political world that one inhabits, and a corresponding shifting in the meanings we then attribute to the very concepts of the 'social', 'political' and 'world'. And this is precisely what is politically significant about the art-work; that is, its capacity to bring into being or think concepts of the 'social' and 'political' that force us to shift our very thinking, that force us to think these notions of 'social' and 'political' differently.

Whether through analysing how Kafka's writings defamiliarize 'law', how Bacon's paintings deterritorialize the 'face' and bring to life an ethics and politics of the body as meat, or how architecture or built form can bring about a shift in our sensibilities regarding the social and political world we inhabit, forcing us to think the 'social' and 'political' differently, Deleuze and Guattari provide us with the resources to think through what I am content to call an *aestheticization of political theory*, where this is taken to imply a critical sensitivity to the productive role that the arts can play in shaping and shifting the meanings we assign to the 'political', and where the arts are invested with an autonomy to think the political as such. The question then becomes: why is it important to argue for the idea that the arts can and should be seen as forms of political theory? This is a question I address explicitly at the end of the conclusion. Here I argue that to emphasize the capacity, indeed autonomy, of aesthetic forms such as literature, painting and architecture in thinking the political – and in thus shifting our sense of what the very term 'political' may mean – is a useful reminder or lesson that political concepts can come in many different forms and that a critical sensitivity to these differences is a crucial acknowledgement of the pluralism of political thought itself.[12]

# 1 • Language and Literature

Deleuze and Guattari immediately force us to confront the idea that there is always-already a politics in the things we name 'language' and 'literature'. And in this chapter my concern will be to render concrete and finesse this basic intuition somewhat, drawing explicitly on two of their works: *A Thousand Plateaus* and *Kafka*.[1] In the first part of the chapter, the focus will be on plateau four of *A Thousand Plateaus*, 'postulates of linguistics', and we will see that Deleuze and Guattari's analysis of 'the postulates of linguistics' is animated by two important and inextricably connected intuitions. First, there is an affirmation of the power of language to intervene directly in social-political life. Second, there is a dismantling of the notion that language finds its primary function in representation: that is, through communication or the exchange of information. We shall encounter terms such as 'indirect discourse', the 'collective assemblage of enunciation', 'incorporeal transformations attributed to bodies', 'order-words' or 'slogans' and we shall see that these Deleuze-Guattarian terms all seek to capture the capacity and power of words to shape and order things in the social-political world. There is a politics immediately and immanently expressed in and through language to the degree that it performs such an ordering function.

In the second and third parts of the chapter, we will turn our attention to Deleuze and Guattari's *Kafka*. For if language has a power and a capacity to order our world, to give shape to our world, to set it in motion in a way that necessarily takes it beyond mere representations or commentaries on the given, then Kafka's body of literary works avail of this power and must, Deleuze and Guattari assert, be thought of as profoundly political. That is to say, Deleuze and Guattari are keen to emphasize that Kafka's writings imply or think a politics that 'experiments' on the real and sets it in motion, effecting a real movement, a defamiliarization or what they call 'deterritorialization' of the world that is itself expressly political. We will turn explicitly in the third and final part of the chapter to this notion of Kafka as a political writer and thinker who 'experiments' on the real. Prior to this, in the second part of the chapter, I will begin with a suggestion or claim that we will see is crucial from Deleuze and Guattari's point of view: namely, that a Kafka politics is intimately connected to his sense of humour or the comic, that 'laughter' is an important key in understanding the political thinking that is expressed in and through the Kafka text. But before all this we must turn to plateau four of *A Thousand Plateaus*, and to the critique of representation immediately implied in and through Deleuze and Guattari's critical engagement with the discipline of linguistics.

## Language, Power, Representation

From the very first sentences of plateau four of *A Thousand Plateaus* Deleuze and Guattari set to work on dismantling the idea that the primary function of language is to represent our world to each other through the communication of information. These sentences are worth quoting at length:

> When the schoolmistress instructs her students on a rule of grammar or arithmetic, she is not informing them, any more than she is informing herself when she questions a student. She does not so much instruct as 'insign', give orders or commands. A teacher's commands are not external or additional to what she teaches. They do not flow from primary signification or result from information: an order always and already concerns prior orders … The compulsory education machine does not communicate information; it imposes upon the child semiotic coordinates possessing all the dual foundations of grammar (masculine-feminine, singular-plural, noun-verb, subject of statement-subject of enunciation, etc.) The elementary unit of language – the statement – is the order-word. Rather than common sense, a faculty for the centralization of information, we must define it as an abominable faculty consisting in emitting, receiving and transmitting order-words. Language is not made to be believed but to be obeyed, and to compel obedience.[2]

We see that Deleuze and Guattari immediately tie language to a social-political institution, 'the compulsory education machine'.

Language has an institutional context and an institutionalizing function. The teacher does not so much inform as give orders. But in what form do these orders come? When Deleuze and Guattari say that orders do not come in the form of commands that are 'external or additional' to what is taught, that an order 'always and already concerns prior orders', they mean to clearly emphasize that a certain ordering or imperative is expressed *immanently* through our use of language. So if I as a teacher (which I flatter myself I am) 'instruct' my students as to the best and most rational way to complete an essay I am not just simply providing information, but am ordering them to do so in a certain way. Therefore, even though my statements may not be explicitly marked or represented by an order or imperative, even though the tone of my discourse may not appear dictatorial or commanding (that is, 'I think it would be best and most rational if you thought about these issues before beginning to draft your essay ...'), this should not detract from the militarism of their functioning. For statements 'always and already concerns prior orders' that are operationalized through my use of, for example, the signifiers of 'best' and 'most rational'. So what could 'best' and 'most rational' mean here? Well, they could mean 'the most convenient and easy thing for me and the students', where 'convenience' expresses certain institutional requirements and realities (the reality that I have a hundred essays to mark in a three week period, the faculty requirement that I need to pass a higher ratio of the essays on this particular module as it seems increasingly bad business to fail fee-paying consumer-students). So in 'instructing' or providing the students with the 'semiotic coordinates' 'best-worst', 'rational-irrational' I, they, and the institution are all swept up and immanently expressed through what at first sight may appear a rather straightforward exchange of information. 'Language', to repeat Deleuze and Guattari's point, 'is not made to be believed but to be obeyed, and to compel obedience'.

So the orders or imperatives that we find in words are not simply marked by an explicit imperative in use ('You must!'), but are expressed immanently, say, for example, through their institutional context (the students ordered and obeying their lecturer, the lecturer ordered and obeying faculty, faculty ordered and obeying the market, meeting their contract with government ...). Although, we need to be careful here in creating the impression that an understanding of language need only fall back on an analysis of its institutional-political context. Deleuze and Guattari are not advocates of the kind of pragmatics that simply views language as a reflection of the institutional, a re-presentation of the 'realities' of institutional-political life. It is just too simple to say that the 'political' (however we would define this most contested of concepts) conditions the linguistic. Against this, Deleuze and Guattari insist that language needs to be approached with a clear sense of its own power, its own capacity to intervene in the thing we may call 'the political', or 'social and political life'. If we go back again to the first few sentences of plateau four quoted above, we can begin to get a sense of this power. As is clear, Deleuze and Guattari want to attribute a central significance to the notion of the 'order-word', calling it the 'the elementary unit of language'.[3] By this they mean that the order-word is a 'function co-extensive with language'; that, simply put, it is fruitless to entertain the idea that language could function without the production of order-words.[4] Thus we can begin to think the power of language as expressed through its functioning as so many order-words. Language orders our world, 'it gives life orders'.[5]

How, then, does language, for Deleuze and Guattari, 'give life orders', or in what way does language have the capacity and power to order our world? The establishment of two key Deleuze-Guattarian intuitions can help clarify matters here. First, language orders our world by operating through what they call *indirect discourse*. Second, language exhibits its capacity or power to intervene in our world by expressing or bringing about *incorporeal transformations on bodies in the social-political field*.

At its simplest, indirect discourse can be thought of as 'hearsay', where language moves by always going from saying to saying. 'We believe,' Deleuze and Guattari argue, 'that narrative consists not in communicating what one has seen but in transmitting what one has heard, what someone else said to you.'[6] Language moves autonomously from saying to saying, subject to subject, person to person. Language can move quite independently from 'we' language-users. Think, for instance, about the seductions and at times the efficacy of cliché. The cliché can be thought of as a useful tool in ordering our world; language as cliché can function to stabilize, even freeze-frame, a world that always has the potential to run away from us via thoughts that fly all over place.[7] My own words as a father of two small children very often fall back on cliché.

Consider the following conversation I recently had with my six-year-old daughter Jessica.

> Why are there police, Daddy?
> To protect us, to keep us safe!
> From bad people?
> What do you mean, bad people?
> Eva said the police are there in case of bad people.
> Well yes, I suppose they are.
> Why are there bad people?
> Dunno.
> Daddy, tell me why people are bad.
> People aren't really bad; they sometimes just do bad things.
> Why?
> Dunno.
> Is it because they weren't loved enough by their mummy or daddy?
> Yes, yes, that's it.
> But you love me and Anna very much Daddy, don't ya?
> Yes sweetie, I love you and your sister very much indeed!

Here Jessica, I and my other four-year-old daughter Anna (whose contribution to the above conversation consisted in a number of very affirmative neck-creaking nods of agreement as each assertion was made) are caught up in an indirect discourse. Hearsay predominates as we are moving from 'saying to saying', cliché to cliché (sometimes consciously, sometimes not). When rationalizing the existence and need for the police ('yes, the police do protect us and keep us safe'), we are not commenting on things we have seen for ourselves, but on things we have heard (a clichéd image of the police absorbed and reiterated unthinkingly). Superficially, it looks as though what we have heard has come from Jessica's friend Eva, but this should and does immediately strike us as ridiculous as this clichéd image of the police belongs to no-one, properly speaking, and reflects a broader intuition or cliché that circulates in the social as such ('yes, the police are necessary … without the enforcement of law and order all would be chaos' … 'yes, we could all do with a good dose of Hobbesian realism when it comes to thinking about these things').[8] Cliché, in this way, speaks through us, being part of an indirect discourse that speaks through us and which helps us order our world accordingly.

Let us come back explicitly to Deleuze and Guattari. Three points are worth emphasizing at this juncture. First, what we may think of as everyday or banal speech action (such as my conversation with Jessica) should be accorded due importance by the student of language. Simply put, the student of language should practise a form of 'pragmatics', where pragmatics traces the internal or intrinsic relations between speech and action (for example, when a promise of love is at once the *action* of *making* a promise).[9] Further still, and Deleuze and Guattari are at their most confrontational here, they want to argue that pragmatics is fundamental to the study of language, and that all the branches of what is sometimes called 'linguistic science' (namely, semantics, syntactics, phonematics etc.) cannot be practised independently of pragmatics. In this way, pragmatics, as Deleuze and Guattari provocatively say, 'becomes the presupposition behind all other dimensions and insinuates itself into everything'.[10] Second, if pragmatics or speech action 'insinuates itself into everything', then any distinction between what linguists would call *langue* and *parole* becomes problematic as the systematicity of the former can no longer be maintained independently of the latter. For instance, speech should not be seen as the extrinsic, individual or context-specific use of a pre-given or already existing syntax, but syntax itself needs to be accounted for by the way it is grounded in speech action.[11] Although, and third, it would obviously be a fundamental mistake to assume that language simply emerges from the speech actor as such, or that it is representative of a fully reflexive and potentially universalizable dialogue between speech actors or subjects.[12] We must remember that language, for Deleuze and Guattari, is an indirect discourse that is essentially impersonal (for example, the inane automatism of the clichéd responses I gave to my daughters, our clichéd image of the police, our unreflexive Hobbesianism ...); that language speaks in and through subjects, rather than being spoken by them. Deleuze and Guattari are quite categorical on this point, and are worth quoting accordingly:

> There is no individual enunciation. There is not even a subject of enunciation. Yet relatively few linguists have analysed the necessarily social character of enunciation ... The social character of enunciation is intrinsically founded only if one succeeds in demonstrating how enunciation in itself implies *collective assemblages*. It then becomes clear that

the statement is individuated, and enunciation subjectified, only to the extent that an impersonal collective assemblage requires it and determines it to be so.[13]

The key concept to emerge here is the 'collective assemblage of enunciation' as this, for Deleuze and Guattari, accounts for the impersonal and social nature of language. A 'collective assemblage of enunciation' implies or implicates itself in language as a series of order-words; of already regulated or patterned actions (again, we could think of my clichéd responses as a paternal figure here); or as the social-institutional environment (for example, the changing market imperatives at play in the 'education' or 'instruction' of fee-paying students in UK universities) in which statements assume force and meaning, or meaning *as* force.[14] Again it is important to emphasize that language is immediately thought to have a force of its own here, a capacity and a power to intervene in and order our world. Deleuze and Guattari are most perspicuous on this point when they directly relate the order-words expressed in and through the 'collective assemblage of enunciation' to what they call the set of all '*incorporeal transformations* current in a given society and *attributed* to the bodies of that society'. With this we see a key distinction emerging between 'the noncorporeal attributes', the 'purely expressed', of the statement or language on the one hand and the 'actions and passions of affected bodies' on the other. Deleuze and Guattari provoke us with a number of examples of such incorporeal transformations, some of which are worth directly citing:

> Peace and war are states or interminglings of very different kinds of bodies, but the declaration of a general mobilization expresses an instantaneous and incorporeal transformation of bodies ... Love is an intermingling of bodies that can be represented by a heart with an arrow through it ... but the declaration 'I love you' expresses a noncorporeal attribute of bodies ... Eating bread and drinking wine are interminglings of bodies; communing with Christ is also an intermingling of bodies ... But the transformation of the body of the bread and the wine into the body and the blood of Christ is the pure expressed of a statement attributed to the bodies. In an airplane hijacking, the threat of a hijacker brandishing a revolver is obviously an action ... But the transformation of the passengers into hostages, and of the plane-body into a prison-body, is an instantaneous incorporeal transformation ...[15]

So, from a Deleuze-Guattarian perspective, language has the purely expressive power and capacity to intervene immediately in the social-political body, to instantaneously and directly change things. Order-words, or what Deleuze and Guattari would also call 'slogans', do not simply re-present the social-political world as function to shape and constitute it in an expressly material way. It is worth noting that this Deleuze-Guattarian critique of representation, their explicit rejection that the language-function is primarily informational or communicational, seems at least initially to motivate them to put a clear question mark against the possibility of reading language ideologically; that is, in accordance with a ready-made concept of ideology. 'Statements definitely do not belong to ideology', and any 'ideological conception of the statement', they claim, 'runs into all kinds of difficulties'.[16] Or, more categorically still, 'There is no ideology and never has been'.[17] What are we to make of a statement such as this? 'There is no ideology and never has been' is an exemplary statement as order-word or slogan. Here the very practice of Deleuze and Guattari's writing embodies the mode of their critical analysis; it is a performative enactment of the critical method they deploy. They sloganize, and in so doing, immediately problematize both the concepts of representation and ideology. How?

First, the slogan needs to be thought in terms of the instantaneousness of its emission, perception and transmission. Rich in perlocutionary effect, the force of the slogan/statement is exerted in a flash.[18] It is almost as if the slogan functions as a kind of lightning flash, striking the eye by distinguishing itself against a background to which it instantly gives a new shape and form. 'There is no ideology and never has been' is a rather dramatic, even audacious, statement given that it assumes its form against a background or a historical tendency to theorize *language as ideology*; say, for example, as the ideological or super-structural re-presentation of a more or less determined economic content.[19] If Deleuze and Guattari's statement can be said to be rich in perlocutionary effect, then this is not because it re-presents something familiar and easily communicable, but precisely because it forces a confusion upon readers who have acquired the habit of politicizing language in accordance with a particular notion of the ideological, one explicitly or even vaguely grounded in terms of the 'economic base' (however subsequently or subtly defined). As someone educated, at least in part, against the historical backcloth of the 'British' adoption and reception of a kind of Althusserianism in political and cultural studies, my own immediate reaction on reading Deleuze and Guattari's statement that there is no ideology and never has been was one of puzzlement and confusion. How can this statement even begin to make sense once we accept the broadly Marxian idea that language itself significantly reflects and represents the socio-economic context of its enunciation? Surely Deleuze and Guattari are caught in the rather debilitating and paradoxical position of supposedly abstracting their statement from any concern with the ideological while using a form of language that has always-already been shaped by the economic-ideological conjuncture that conditions it from the very first instance? It was with the invention of this type of rhetorical question that I dismissed Deleuze and Guattari's statement that there is no ideology and never has been.[20]

This dismissal of Deleuze and Guattari's statement/slogan can be subsequently viewed as somewhat premature, especially if we become sensitive to the specific conjuncture it illuminates and reshapes (for example, my rather vague and unthinking Althusserianism, my clinging to the representationalist base/superstructure model they are seeking to dismantle).[21] This brings us to a second characteristic of the slogan, what Deleuze and Guattari would call its 'power of forgetting'. For if the slogan/statement is an instantaneous lightning flash, then its duration and intensity is limited to the conjuncture or the social body to which it is attributed. There is an implicit functionalism in this. To repeat: a slogan/statement does not represent something, or mean something, as much as it functions by intervening in the social body. A slogan is not a claim to transcendence or universality, so much as a singularly useful intervention that changes things. So, it would be misplaced to judge Deleuze and Guattari's statement that 'There is no ideology and never has been' as a transcendental or universal claim, and to oppose it with an equally transcendental or universal intuition that there is always ideology and always has been.[22] To assume Deleuze and Guattari are claiming that ideology is a totally useless concept now and always, that any critical analysis of social-political life must be conditioned or always-already predicated on a dismissal of the notion of ideology, simply misses the point of their sloganizing as such. The 'power of forgetting' in the slogan is a singular power that allows only for a certain movement or change in things, that allows us to forget in order to move on, 'permitting one to feel absolved' of the slogans 'one has followed and abandoned', and 'to welcome new ones'.[23]

It should come as no surprise, then, that Deleuze and Guattari in a later passage of *A Thousand Plateaus* entertain the possibility of revamping or moving the concept of ideology in a new direction. 'The only way to ... revamp the theory of ideology [is] by saying that expressions and statements intervene directly in productivity, in the form of a production of meaning or sign-value.'[24] By intervening directly in the production of meaning or sign-value, we could say that language or the statement/slogan has a certain ideological power or capacity to produce meaning, to force meaning in this way or that. Thereby a critique of ideology would not focus on the supposedly superstructural or epiphenomenal expression of any reflected or re-presented economic-social content, but would locate itself at the very heart of meaning-production itself. As I have argued elsewhere, Deleuze and Guattari do indeed engage in this kind of critique of ideology in *Anti-Oedipus* by challenging what we would call the 'Oedipalization of desire' in psychoanalysis.[25] The basic point is this: psychoanalysis is ideological to the extent that it produces meaning as desire expressed through 'lack' (that is, desire is seen as a reactive response to an unsatisfied want or lost object); to the degree that it fabricates or constructs 'lack' in or through the social relations of the contemporary polity. Meaning as 'lack' is anchored in the process of production quite explicitly, for Deleuze and Guattari, precisely because it structures desire in accordance with the wants, needs or values of the dominant class in the contemporary market economy. Or as they explicitly put it: 'The deliberate creation of lack as a function of market economy is the art of a dominant class'.[26]

By structuring or making desire function around an idea of 'lack', by implicitly suggesting that desire is a reactive response to an unsatisfied want or persistently lacking object, psychoanalysis provides the perfect *raison d'être* for capitalist consumption and production. Psychoanalysis, in other words, literally teaches us to desire by instilling in us the fear and anxiety that our 'wants' and 'needs' are not yet satisfied and this, Deleuze and Guattari insist, generates on behalf of the 'dominant' capitalist class ever more economic production and consumption.[27] So, in this sense, 'Oedipus'

– the term Deleuze and Guattari attribute to the discourse of psychoanalysis – connects explicitly to the social formation that is contemporary capitalism. Deleuze and Guattari write or, should we say, 'sloganize' as follows:

> Only in appearance is Oedipus a beginning, either as a historical or prehistorical origin, or as a structural foundation. In reality it is a completely ideological beginning, for the sake of ideology. Oedipus is always and solely an aggregate of destination fabricated to meet the requirements of an aggregate of departure constituted by a social formation.[28]

To sloganize Deleuze-Guattari style is immediately to problematize and critique the idea that language finds its primary function in representation; to sloganize Deleuze-Guattari style is immediately to affirm the power of language to intervene in our world in an expressly material way. A word such as 'ideology' cannot simply be represented by way of a meaning that is transcendentally conditioned and universally applicable ('This is what the signifier ideology means, and this is why it will always mean this ...!'). Rather it is pragmatically connected to a form of language-use that plugs it into varying conjunctures/bodies. This is why there is no necessary contradiction in Deleuze and Guattari seemingly dismissing the efficacy of 'ideology' as a critical tool ('There is no ideology and never has been') while then using it in their critique of psychoanalysis (Oedipus as ideology, 'for the sake of ideology'). Of course, we may be tempted to say that Deleuze and Guattari are simply rejecting one theory of ideology (that is, the representationalist or base/superstructure model which understands ideology to be a reflection of an always-already given economic-social content) and suggesting another (where ideology directly intervenes in meaning-production, where language has its own ideological power to force meaning in this way or that). But this already assumes too much by overlooking the important extent to which pragmatics 'insinuates itself into everything'. We assume the word is subject to a law of identity, say semantically, and rather casually forget that pragmatically speaking it is subject to continual variation every time it performs its meaning-production function. Put simply, the word 'ideology' as it appears on page 101 of *Anti-Oedipus* is an altogether different word to the one that appears initially on page 4 of *A Thousand Plateaus*.[29]

As has been argued throughout the first part of this chapter, Deleuze and Guattari's analysis of 'the postulates of linguistics' is animated by two important and inextricably connected intuitions that are worthy of attention. There is an affirmation of the power of language to intervene directly in social-political life, and a dismantling of the notion that language finds its primary function in representation: that is, through communication or the exchange of information. 'Indirect discourse', the 'collective assemblage of enunciation', 'incorporeal transformations attributed to bodies' are Deleuze-Guattarian terms that all seek to capture the capacity and power of words to shape and order things in the social-political world. There is a politics immediately and immanently expressed in language to the degree that it performs such an ordering function. We could call this ordering function, this power, 'ideology', but only if we take care to suffuse the word 'ideology' with the power or potential to internally and pragmatically differentiate itself in accordance with the conjunctures/bodies to which it is connected. Or we might want to go in a different direction, perform another move, and think the power of language as so many 'experiments' on a world that is never simply just represented, but a world, a reality, that it always sets in motion. In a different context, in their work on Kafka, Deleuze and Guattari do indeed perform this very move. Here they seek to show how Kafka's use of language, how Kafka's body of 'literary' works, implies and thinks a politics that 'experiments' on the real and sets the world in motion. We will turn explicitly in the third and final part of the chapter to this notion of Kafka as a political writer and thinker who 'experiments' on the real. For the moment, though, or in the next part of the chapter, I will begin with a suggestion or claim that we will see is crucial from Deleuze and Guattari's point of view: namely, that a Kafka politics is intimately connected to his sense of humour or the comic, that 'laughter' is an important key in understanding the political thinking expressed in and through the Kafka text.

## Kafka as a Comic and Political Writer

In one crucial passage at the end of chapter four of *Kafka*, Deleuze and Guattari offer two key principles that they feel should animate the analysis of Kafka's work. Kafka, they strongly assert, needs to be approached as a writer who is at once political and comic. He is from start to finish a political author and a comic author, a writer who expresses profound laughter and joy, a laughter and joy that are themselves profoundly political. The passage in question is really rather long and, dare I say, typically Deleuze-Guattarian by the way it packs in or condenses a proliferating series of statements and claims that provoke the reader. But it is a passage that is worth quoting at length, and one that merits, and will indeed reward, some attention. It reads as follows:

> Only one thing really bothers Kafka and angers him, makes him indignant: when people treat him as a writer of intimacy, finding a refuge in literature, as an author of solitude, of guilt, of an intimate misfortune. However, that's really Kafka's fault, since he held out that interpretation in order to anticipate the trap through his humour. There is a Kafka laughter, a very joyous laughter, that people usually understand poorly … Only two principles are necessary to accord with Kafka. He is an author who laughs with a profound joy, a *joie de vivre*, in spite of, or because of, his own clownish declarations that he offers like a trap or a circus. And from one end to the other, he is a political author, prophet of the future world, because he has two poles that he will know how to unify in a completely new assemblage: far from a being a writer withdrawn into his room, Kafka finds that his room offers him a double flux, that of a bureaucrat with a great future ahead of him, plugged into real assemblages that are in the process of coming into shape, and that of a nomad who is involved in fleeing things in the most contemporary way and who plugs into socialism, anarchism, social movements. Writing for Kafka, the primacy of writing, signifies only one thing: not a form of literature alone, the enunciation forms a unity with desire, beyond laws, states, regimes. Yet the enunciation is always historical, political, and social. A micropolitics, a politics of desire that questions all situations. Never has there been a more comic and joyous author from the point of view of desire; never has there been a more political and social author from the point of view of enunciation. Everything leads to laughter, starting with *The Trial*. Everything is political, starting with the letters to Felice.[30]

The merit of quoting this passage at such length is two fold. First, and perhaps most obviously, it contains many of the key intuitions that Deleuze and Guattari carry with them to the Kafka text, and it will be necessary to begin setting about exploring some of these throughout the rest of the chapter. Second, it again details for us Deleuze and Guattari's 'style' of argumentation, which is condensed to be sure, but more importantly is direct, immediate, polemical, provocative and challenging – in short, they are sloganizing again! They are expressing a series of statements that singularly intervene on a body that is itself given new or different attributes, a body shifted, reshaped, disrupted or even defamiliarized. The body in question here is, of course, the body of Kafka scholarship as such. The polemical tone or tenor of Deleuze and Guattari's remarks immediately strikes us as they warn against certain potential dead-ends characteristic of a scholarship that would seek to separate art and life in Kafka. Strictly speaking, there is no maintainable distinction to be made between Kafka's life as an artist or writer and the life that pulses through his writing as such.[31] It is a profound political mistake seemingly to detect or, much worse, institutionalize a form of public/private split (to steal a choice phrase from feminist thought)[32] in Kafka, where somehow a Kafka biography of, say, individual and asocial impotence (for instance, the image of Kafka as an impotent lonely figure shut away in his room at night, writing to take refuge from a world that he cannot really function in, Kafka the grown man who writes to compensate for a life of impotence and inaction, a man who never marries, who never stands up to a dominating or overbearing father ...) is represented or is read directly onto his work, a body of work that is then assumed to be disconnected from the social as such precisely because of the individualized and atomized conditions of its enunciation.[33]

This kind of reading, for Deleuze and Guattari, 'bothers Kafka' and rightly makes him 'indignant', but it also implicates him as he invites such stupid responses by holding out the bait. It is, as they say, 'really Kafka's fault, since he held out that interpretation in order to anticipate the trap through his humour'. So we see that two claims are being run together and developed by Deleuze and Guattari in the first two sentences of the passage above. First, it is a mistake to view Kafka as an isolated figure whose work or writing is merely the externalization of his loneliness, impotence, sickness. Second, Kafka himself potentially lures us into the trap of such stupidities by inviting this interpretation. And this interpretation is, properly speaking, humourless or, better still, fails Kafka by failing to be sensitive to the particular kind of humour that Kafka injects into his writing. What kind of humour are we talking about here? In chapter two of *Kafka*, Deleuze and Guattari invite us to consider his now infamous 'Letter to the Father'.[34] The tragedy of this letter is that it is grist to the mill of so many individualizing and consequently depoliticizing readings: 'so many unfortunate psychoanalytic interpretations'.[35] Just as Deleuze and Guattari seek strongly and polemically to oppose psychoanalysis and the 'Oedipalization of desire' in *Anti-Oedipus*, so too do they want to combat the 'Oedipalization of desire' in *Kafka*. From a Deleuze-Guattarian perspective, it is only if we suspend our sense of humour, or read Kafka in a humourless fashion, that we can then proceed with any kind of psychoanalytical or Oedipalizing story. The story trades on the following stupidities or banalities: (1) Kafka suffers at the hands of a father who never stops judging him and makes him feel guilty; (2) Kafka internalizes this guilt, only to return the gesture and accuse the father of guilt in judging and undermining him; (3) so everything then becomes the fault of the father – shyness, impotence, flight from the world through writing, not marrying ..., can all be blamed on him. As we said, Deleuze and Guattari would clearly see this narrative in terms of an 'Oedipalization of desire', or as the construction 'of a classic Oedipus of the neurotic sort, where the beloved father is hated, accused, and declared to be guilty'.[36]

This Oedipalizing or psychoanalytical story leaves no room for absurdity, humour, the kind of comic exaggeration of the Oedipal father-figure that is expressed in Kafka's writing. At one point in 'Letter to the Father', Kafka precisely provides an image of the father that is expanded and exaggerated to the point of absurdity, a gigantic father projected across the whole world, an Oedipal figure with an almost universal reach.[37] This comic exaggeration of Oedipus, this 'Oedipalization of the universe' as Deleuze and Guattari say, importantly implies the 'sort of microscopic enlargement' that 'shows up the father for what he is; it gives him a *molecular agitation in which an entirely different sort of combat is being played out*'.[38] In other words, there is what Deleuze and Guattari would call a *becoming-molecular* in Kafka's writing which is both comic and political, expressed through the construction of the absurd image of the Oedipal figure who, when microscopically analysed, is then revealed as a product of a certain combat or regime of power. So before there is Oedipus (for example, the gesture of blame, of attributing guilt to the Oedipal figure to explain one's own impotence) there is power, the institutionalization of a neurotic desire for the kind of 'lack' that Deleuze and Guattari analyse and connect to consumer capitalism in *Anti-Oedipus*. Or, as they more bluntly put it in *Kafka*, 'In short, it's not Oedipus that produces neurosis; it is neurosis – *that is, a desire that is already submissive and searching to communicate its own submission* – that produces Oedipus. Oedipus the market value of neurosis.' [39] Beginning to come into view here is what Deleuze and Guattari refer to in the passage above as Kafka's 'micropolitics', his 'politics of desire'. We could again connect this to Deleuze and Guattari's sustained challenge to any public/private split in Kafka. For Kafka's 'micropolitics' or 'politics of desire' immediately connects the supposedly private realm of the familial (father, son, mother, sister relations) to the political; or, better still, his is a literature that always-already sees and thinks the political as pulsing through the familial, agitating it, shaping its desire in relation to power.[40] We could consider, in this regard, what is perhaps Kafka's most famous short story, 'The Metamorphosis'.[41]

As is well known, the story begins with what at first sight may seem a rather fantastical or spectacular revelation: a man, Gregor Samsa, awakens from troubled dreams to find himself transformed into an insect.[42] From a Deleuze-Guattarian perspective, there is nothing necessarily fantastical or spectacular in this, nothing symbolic, nothing metaphorical. They argue that Gregor Samsa's transformation is not meaningful or significant because it can be read symbolically, metaphorically or allegorically (for example, as an effect of guilt on the subject, the imaginary objectification of guilt or self-loathing). Rather, the provocation of the transformation, the provocation of 'The Metamorphosis' as a story, the provocation of Kafka's short stories as a whole, is that they express what Deleuze and Guattari call a 'becoming-animal' that is *real*: that is, a real potential to chart a genuine escape from the cramped space of a familial sphere that has a tendency to close in on itself. Deleuze and Guattari write:

> There is nothing metaphoric about the becoming-animal. No symbolism, no allegory. Nor is it the result of a flaw or a malediction, the effect of some sort of guilt ... It is a map of intensities. It is an ensemble of states, each distinct from the other, grafted onto the man in so far as he is searching for a way out. It is a creative line of escape that says nothing other than what it is ... [T]he becoming-animal ... constitutes a single process, a unique method that replaces subjectivity.[43]

So Gregor encounters himself as a new body and it is interesting to note that from the first sentences of the story Kafka is concerned to foreground the materiality of the bodily transformation as we learn that he is 'lying on his hard shell-like back', that by lifting his head a little Gregor 'could see his curved brown belly, divided by stiff arching ribs', how his 'numerous legs, which were pathetically thin compared to the rest of his bulk, danced helplessly before his eyes'.[44] The problem initially posed by 'The Metamorphosis' is immediately fleshy and material, and the 'becoming-animal' that Deleuze and Guattari see in this story needs to be approached in light of this 'fleshy materialism'.[45] As Deleuze and Guattari say, 'becoming-animal' at once signals the potential for escape, for new 'intensities', affirming the capacity and power of bodies to do new things. Indeed, we learn from Kafka of the new intensive states or bodily capacities that Gregor is capable of experiencing as he particularly 'enjoyed hanging from the ceiling; it was quite different from lying on the floor; one could breathe more freely ...'.[46] It is as if the materiality of the bodily transformation immediately counters any sense that Gregor is merely dreaming, that he is caught up in a fantasy, something imaginary. Again and again Kafka dispels this notion:

> 'Suppose I went back to sleep for a little and forgot all this nonsense', [Gregor] thought, but that was utterly impracticable for he was used to sleeping on his right side and in his present state he was unable to get into that position. However vigorously he swung himself to the right he kept rocking on to his back again. He must have tried it a hundred times, he shut his eyes so as not to have to watch his struggling legs, and only left off when he began to feel a faint dull ache in his side which was entirely new to him.[47]

In coming back specifically to Kafka's 'micropolitics', his 'politics of desire', two Deleuze-Guattarian points are immediately worth considering. First, there is a hint, a suggestion, of a politics expressed through 'becoming-animal' as a 'creative line of escape'. To the extent that this 'becoming-animal' expresses or accords with the body's capacity to experience new intensive states, to do new things or enter into new relations, then this politics has, for Deleuze in particular, a certain ethical resonance and significance. Those familiar with Deleuze's work will instantly recognize the importance of his writings on Spinoza here, for in books such as *Spinoza: Practical Philosophy* and, more extensively still, *Expressionism in Philosophy: Spinoza*, Deleuze develops the notion of an 'ethics of joy' that is grounded precisely in the capacity of the body to enter into new relations.[48] However, and secondly from a Deleuze-Guattarian perspective, this kind of ethics and politics never fully materializes in Kafka's 'The Metamorphosis', or in his short stories more generally, as the 'becoming-animal' as a 'creative line of escape' remains blocked, or becomes too cramped by the familial unit that closes in on itself.[49]

How, then, does this happen in 'The Metamorphosis'? What is important here is the way in which certain political-economic imperatives play themselves in and through the familial unit, how they become institutionalized in the familial unit as such, and how, as a consequence, the familial unit cramps, becomes agitated, and ultimately desires to close in on itself. Gregor's 'becoming-animal' comes to express a profound loss rather than being seen as a potential for creative escape, and the loss is from first to last a political-economic one. We note from the above passage that Gregor shuts his eyes, averting his gaze from the sight of his struggling legs. Why does Gregor refuse to contemplate himself? To be sure, Kafka plays with the image of the insect as an object of disgust, even self-loathing, but the answer we are given to this question is one which more readily plugs us into the machinery of capital immanent to the constitution of the familial unit. Gregor, now being an insect, can no longer work and his father, mother and sister all take jobs in an attempt to make up for the loss of income. In short, the metamorphosis precipitates a proletarianization of the Samsa family.[50] The familial unit is quite literally replaced at the dinner table by capital, or at least by the promise of it from the three lodgers who now occupy their home. Gregor watches them through a crack in the door:

They seated themselves at the top end of the table, where in the old days his father and mother and Gregor had sat, unfolded their napkins, and picked up their knives and forks. At once his mother appeared in the doorway with a dish of meat, and close behind her his sister, bearing a dish piled high with potatoes. Thick clouds of steam rose from the food. The lodgers bent over the dishes that were set in front of them, as if they wished to examine them before eating, and in fact the one sitting in the middle, who seemed to be regarded as an authority by the other two, sliced into a piece of meat while it was still on the dish, evidently to determine whether it was sufficiently tender or whether perhaps it should be returned to the kitchen. He was satisfied, and both mother and sister, who had been watching anxiously, breathed again freely and began to smile.[51]

From a Deleuze-Guattarian perspective, this passage of writing is vintage Kafka, from beginning to end both comical and political. The humour is clearly expressed through the comic exaggeration of the power of the authority figures, and this is pushed to the point of absurdity (in particular, the rather absurd paternal figure of the 'middle' lodger 'who seemed to be regarded as an authority by the other two'). The politics is expressed and thought through what we could again call the construction of the *becoming-molecular* of the absurd figure, a figure revealed to be the product of a certain combat or regime of power. Here the figure of the lodger condenses the economic-political forces outside, but pulsing through, the familial unit, forces which agitate and shape its desire to submit to power ('I hope the meat is tender enough …', 'I hope the potatoes are hot enough …',). When Kafka says: 'He was satisfied, and both mother and sister, who had been watching anxiously, breathed again freely and began to smile', he is inviting us as readers to engage a smile of our own, a political smile that ends in laughter in the face of the absurd, a comic amplification that forces the familial unit under a microscope and, in so doing, connects it to the economic forces that traverse and shape it.[52]

If the politics of 'becoming-animal' expressed through the short stories are ultimately truncated or blocked (for example, the Samsa family kill and get rid of Gregor whose presence is, in the end, intolerable to them),[53] then the broader political significance of Kafka's writing would seem to lie elsewhere. Such is the importance, then, of the novels for Deleuze and Guattari. For it is in and through the 'unfinished novels' – *The Trial, The Castle, America* – that Kafka's politics assumes a fuller sense and significance. Again we can go back to the Deleuze-Guattarian passage we initially quoted from the end of chapter four of *Kafka*. Here, Kafka is described as a 'political author' to the extent that he is a 'nomad who is involved in fleeing things in the most contemporary way and who plugs into socialism, anarchism, social movements', practising a style of writing or 'enunciation' that forms a 'unity with desire, beyond laws, states, regimes', a 'micropolitics, a politics of desire that questions all situations'. So, Kafka's writing or 'enunciation' connects to desire and constitutes a 'politics of desire' that questions the law, the state, regimes of power and, in the process, plugs into 'social movements' that seek to do the same. In other words, Kafka's 'literary machine', as Deleuze and Guattari call it, exhibits the capacity to question and critique regimes of power, particularly as they begin to circulate around law and the state apparatus. More needs to be said about this notion of social and political critique.

## Kafka, Critique, Representation

In what is perhaps the pivotal chapter in *Kafka*, chapter five 'Immanence and Desire', Deleuze and Guattari importantly caution against a representationalist reading of Kafka's politics; that is, one which understands social and political critique in Kafka to be a part of a politics of representation as such. If Kafka is a realist, then this for Deleuze and Guattari is a realism anchored not so much in a fidelity to the real as represented, but rather in a form of writing and thinking that 'experiments' on the real, defamiliarizing it and making it take flight. Again it is worth quoting Deleuze and Guattari at length in order to begin to get a feel for the intuitions or assumptions anchoring their argument. They write:

> So, should we support realist and social interpretations of Kafka? Certainly, since they are infinitely closer to noninterpretation … One could object that Kafka's America is unreal, that the New York strike remains intangible, that the most difficult working conditions receive no indignation in his work, that the election of the judge falls into the

realm of pure nonsense. One might correctly note that there is never any criticism in Kafka ... In *The Trial*, K doesn't attack the law and willingly aligns himself with ... the executioners ... In *The Castle*, K likes to menace and punish whenever he can. Can we conclude that, not being a 'critic of his time', Kafka turned his criticism 'against himself' and had no other tribunal than an 'internal tribunal'? This would be grotesque, since it would turn criticism into a dimension of representation ... Kafka attempts to extract from social representations assemblages of enunciation and machinic assemblages ... [I]n the novels, the dismantling of the assemblages makes the social representation take flight in a much more effective way than a critique would have done and brings about a deterritorialization of the world that is itself political ...[54]

Four related points or intuitions follow from what Deleuze and Guattari are saying here, or they can be extrapolated from the passage with relative ease. First, supporting a realist and social-political interpretation of Kafka implies sensitivity concerning how his writing, his use of language, operates by intervening directly in the social body. And this, Deleuze and Guattari would argue, has less do with the 'interpretation' or re-presentation of meaning, than with an analysis of its function. Pushed toward 'noninterpretation', then, we are moved only by the problem of how Kafka's literary machine singularly works by intervening in the social-political field. Second, and being pushed toward 'noninterpretation', it becomes problematic to ground Kafka's politics by mere resource to communicable narrative content, as this fails to capture the singular power of his writing. This, for example, is why Deleuze and Guattari dismiss the objection that Kafka's description or representation of America is unrealistic, why they think that such objections are of little importance. Therefore, 'there is never any criticism' in Kafka if by 'criticism' we seek to attribute to his work some documentary function whereby the representations found in narrative content (for example, the descriptions of America) are thought to function as an external commentary of the situation represented. Therefore, and this is the third point, Kafka does not comment on social-political life by way of representations that can be judged to be more or less accurate; rather his writing operates by extracting from 'social representations assemblages of enunciation and machinic assemblages'. This, fourth and most importantly, is expressed in the novels through the 'dismantling of the assemblages', leading to a situation where 'social representations' take flight, where 'critique' gives way to a 'deterritorialization of the world that is itself political'.

Of course, stated in this rather flat manner, these intuitions beg any number of questions. For example, are Deleuze and Guattari simply arguing that Kafka's writing fails to embody any workable notion of social and political critique? Or is it important to understand their remarks in light of a critique of any image of critique grounded in representation, and communicated through external commentary? And how would such a critique (that is, one not grounded in representation) work anyway? In other words, how does the critical gesture of extracting 'assemblages of enunciation and machinic assemblages' from 'social representations' express the 'dismantling of the assemblages' as such, and how does this practice of critique make 'social representations' take flight by way of a 'deterritorialization of the world that is itself political'?

We should immediately note that by connecting or translating social representations into assemblages Kafka is, for Deleuze and Guattari, always-already dismantling them. 'Writing,' say Deleuze and Guattari, 'has a double function: to translate everything into assemblages and to dismantle the assemblages. The two are the same thing.' [55] In what sense, then, is translation and dismantling the same thing? Consider, for example, the way in which the problem of the 'law' is posed or 'represented' in *The Trial*. Earlier we showed how there was a kind of becoming-molecular in Kafka's letters and short stories, a comic exaggeration of Oedipal or authority figures (Kafka's father, or the lodgers in 'The Metamorphosis'), which simultaneously operates as a political critique of a certain desire to submit to power (recall, for instance, the desire of Gregor's mother and sister that dinner meets with the expectation and approval of the lodgers occupying their home). In *The Trial*, or in the 'unfinished novels' more generally, this political critique of represented figures of power or authority becomes ever more complicated. Most immediately, we see Kafka constantly connecting and translating law into a social situation and bureaucratic apparatus that is weirdly unfamiliar or defamiliarizing. As Ronald Bogue puts it, 'Kafka defamiliarizes the Law by depriving it of its conventional, commonsense logic'.[56] In other words, the law appears to be without any discernible form, or a form with no

concrete content, K's guilt seems assumed, charges remain unspeci-
fied, bureaucratic or legal structures remain opaque, inaccessible,
the familiar commonsense notions that inform our representation
and recognition of the law as law to ourselves and others – for
example, that law be governed by reason and reasoned argument,
that legal judgments are grounded on the basis of proof and
evidence, that the law be transparent and accessible to all, that
guilt can never be presumed – all seem to give way to 'a byzantine
mechanism of power ... regulated by a hierarchy of forces, a
presumption of universal culpability and an inescapable network
of punitive agents'.[57]

So by translating law into an assemblage of punitive power, by
defamiliarizing law in this way, Kafka provides a critique of law as
power, or at least a way of beginning to dismantle any received
notion of law as ethically anchored in, say, certain 'democratic'
values. It is in this sense that Kafka's translation of law into power
is simultaneously its dismantling. Where we tend to think of law as
accessible and near to hand, Kafka emphasizes, as Deleuze and
Guattari say, 'the transcendence of the law', a projected image of
the law as 'negative theology', a kind of 'theology of absence'.[58]
Again and again Kafka confronts us with the idea that the law, like
the God of negative theology, is ultimately unknowable, and can
be materially expressed only through the edict literally inscribed
on the body. 'In the Penal Colony', to take an obvious example,
confronts us with a law machine, the needles of which inscribe the
sentence of the body of the accused.[59] Where we tend to think of
law as anchored in a state apparatus that is forbidden to encroach
on our freedom unless and until we are found guilty of any crime,
Kafka emphasizes the 'a prioriness of guilt', again a quasi-theolog-
ical notion that we are always-already guilty in advance.[60] Now,
while this translation of the law into a form of negative theology is
clearly a present and dominant theme in short stories such as 'In
The Penal Colony' or 'The Great Wall of China', it finds its most
sustained and definitive treatment in *The Trial*, and in particular
the chapter entitled 'In the Cathedral'.[61] This chapter, the penulti-
mate chapter of the book, the one preceding K's execution in the
concluding chapter, has been accorded significance and importance
by those Kafka scholars who seek to emphasize the religious char-
acter of the book.[62] But, for Deleuze and Guattari, this chapter of
*The Trial* remains 'highly ambiguous' and they stress that a critical

sensitivity is needed here to appreciate how the supposedly religious themes actually give way to profoundly political ones. They read Kafka's translation of the law into negative theology and his critique of law as punitive and scripturally sanctioned power as only a preliminary gesture, which then enables him to construct or think a different type of social-political critique. They argue:

> [I]t is less a question of presenting this image of a transcendental and unknowable law than of *dissecting the mechanism* of an entirely different sort of machine, which needs this image of the law only to align its gears and make them function together ... *The Trial* must be considered ... a report of the experiments on the functioning of a machine in which the law runs the strong risk of playing no more than the role of exterior armature. That's why ... *The Trial* should be used only with great care ...[63]

Earlier we said that Kafka is a writer and thinker whose writings constituted a series of experiments on the real, implying that this experimentation carries with it a politics or form of political critique. And this is clearly what Deleuze and Guattari are suggesting here in their description of *The Trial* as a 'report of the experiments on the functioning of a machine in which the law runs the strong risk of playing no more than the role of exterior armature'. But how does this experimentation express itself in *The Trial*? And what kind of political thinking or political critique emerges from this text or from the 'In the Cathedral' chapter in particular? Before beginning to answer these questions it is clearly necessary to delve into the text and this chapter in more detail. Here K, the accused, encounters a 'priest', a functionary of the court, who attempts to shed some light on the meaning and significance of the law. K is intent on listening and learning for, even though he is suspicious of the court, K trusts the priest and tells him so. The priest reproaches K for 'deluding' himself about the nature of the court and the law – a 'delusion' he tries to illustrate by way of a story or parable.

Before the law, the priest tells K, is a doorkeeper. To this doorkeeper comes a man who seeks entrance to the law. The doorkeeper refuses entry to the man. The man enquires as to whether he will be allowed in at some point in the future. 'It is possible,' the doorkeeper says, 'but not at this moment.' The doorkeeper, seeing the man attempting to peer through the entrance and feeling that perhaps he may be lured into trying to enter without permission, warns against the difficulties that will be encountered. He laughs condescendingly and says: 'If you are so strongly tempted, try to get in without my permission. But note that I am powerful. And I am only the lowest doorkeeper. From hall to hall, keepers stand at every door, one more powerful than the other. Even the third of these has an aspect than even I cannot bear to look at.'[64]

The man is puzzled. The law, he has always thought, should be universally accessible, 'to every man, and at all times'. Considering the doorkeeper a rather imposing figure and in light of his declaration, the man decides to wait to get permission to enter. He waits and waits ... days, months, years pass. During this time, the man attempts on many occasions to bribe the doorkeeper with the valuables he had brought for his journey. The doorkeeper does indeed accept these gifts, but remains unmoved. On receipt of each gift he says: 'I take this only to keep you from feeling you have left something undone'.[65] Over time the man's eyes grow dim, but in the darkness he can perceive a radiance emanating from the door of the law. The man's life is drawing to a close. Before dying, all that he has experienced thus far, the priest tells K, seems to condense into a single question: 'Everyone strives for the law, how does it come about', the man asks, 'that in all these years no one has come seeking admittance but me?'. The doorkeeper responds: 'No one but you could gain admittance through this door, since this door was intended only for you. I am now going to shut it'.[66]

Coming back to Deleuze and Guattari, it is obviously important to analyse what is happening in 'In the Cathedral' in political terms, as the priest's role, being a functionary of the court, is a political one, and that the construction or translation of the law into a 'negative theology' occurring through the parable has significance only to the extent that it functions politically to subjugate K. Put simply, law can assume the extra-legal and political power to subjugate in so far as it is made to *appear* transcendentally unknowable. We learn from Kafka that K is 'strongly attracted to the story', but that he immediately concludes that the doorkeeper deludes the man by giving him the message of salvation – that is, telling him the door was meant for him – only when it could no longer help him. The political consequences of such an interpretation are obvious enough. The worst thing K can do is to stand awestruck before the law or its representatives (for instance, the priest). The priest responds to K's initial interpretation by way of a reproach: 'Don't be too hasty', he says, 'don't take over an opinion without testing it'.[67] He then sets to work on K, robbing him of the impetus for questioning by presenting him with a series of supposedly well argued interpretations that seem to throw the 'meaning' of the parable itself into question.[68] Immediately, the priest blocks the idea that the doorkeeper – the law's representative – is culpable. K is reproached by the priest for not having 'enough respect for the written word' and 'for altering the story' for his own ends. The parable, the priest tells K, contains two important statements concerning the admission to the law. At the beginning, the doorkeeper says that he cannot admit the man at that moment; at the end, he says the door was meant only for him. There is no contradiction here, the priest tells K. Indeed the first statement, according to the priest's interpretation, even implies the second one. The priest even stretches things to say that the doorkeeper may have been exceeding his duty in suggesting the possibility of further admittance. The priest also feels the necessity to point out that the doorkeeper never leaves his post in all these years; that he does not shut the door until the very last moment; that he is conscious of the importance of his office ('I am powerful') but at the same time expresses a respect for his superiors ('I am only the lowest doorkeeper'); that he refuses to be corrupted, accepting the man's gifts only to keep from him the feeling of having left 'something undone'.[69]

With these and other arguments the priest begins to paint a picture of the doorkeeper as a dutiful, if somewhat simple and slightly conceited, servant of the law. The priest, through the power of his arguments and from the authority that comes from an exacting analysis of scripture, forces K to concede his initial thoughts. K deferentially responds to the priest: 'You have studied the story more exactly and for a longer time than I have'. K is silenced, and breaks his silence only to seek out another judgment from the priest. He asks: 'So you think the man was not deluded?' 'Don't misunderstand me,' says the priest, 'I am only showing you the various opinions concerning the point ... The scriptures are unalterable and the comments often enough merely express the commentator's bewilderment. In this case there even exists an interpretation which claims the deluded person is really the doorkeeper.' [70] This immediately strikes K as fanciful and 'far fetched'. Yet, perhaps in the knowledge that he has already been humbled by the priest, he does not dismiss the interpretation and calls instead for clarification.

The priest bases this argument on the 'simple-mindedness' of the doorkeeper, the suggestion being that he does not know the law from the inside, that he knows only the way that leads to it, and how to patrol it. His concept of the interiority of the law is, in this regard, taken to be childish. Although it is said by some commentators, the priest tells K, that he must have in some sense been privy to the interior; that a servant of the law must be appointed from the inside. However, this argument is countered, we are told, by the suggestion that he may have been appointed from a voice calling from the interior. It must also be borne in mind, the priest tells K, that the aspect of the third doorkeeper is more than he can endure. In this regard, he could not have penetrated the law by a great deal. From this perspective, the priest claims that the ignorance of the doorkeeper with respect to the interiority of the law is evidence enough to suggest the possibility that he is in a state of delusion.

Again we find the priest able, with these and other arguments, to impress and impose himself on K. After having repeated to himself in a low voice several passages from the above exposition, K finds himself in agreement with the priest and in light of this tries to reformulate his initial thoughts. He says:

> It is well argued, and I am inclined to agree that the doorkeeper is deluded. But this has not made me abandon my former opinion, since both conclusions are to some extent compatible. Whether the doorkeeper is clear-sighted or deluded does not dispose of the matter. I said the man is deluded. If the doorkeeper ... is deluded, then his delusion must of necessity be communicated to the man. That makes the doorkeeper not, indeed, a swindler, but a creature so simple minded that he ought to be dismissed at once from his office. You mustn't forget that the doorkeeper's delusions do himself no harm but do infinite harm to the man. [71]

Immediately the priest questions the conclusions drawn by K. He objects to the idea of passing judgement on the doorkeeper. 'Many aver,' he says, 'that the story confers no right on anyone to pass judgement on the doorkeeper. Whatever he may seem to us, he is yet a servant of the Law; that is, he belongs to the Law and as such is set beyond human judgment ...: to doubt his integrity is to doubt the Law itself.'[72] At once K disagrees; the acceptance of such a conclusion, he says, necessitates that we accept everything the doorkeeper says as true, an impossibility in light of what has already been said about the nature of his delusion. 'No,' the priest retorts, 'it is not necessary to accept everything as true, one must only accept it as necessary.' 'A melancholy conclusion', says K. 'It turns lying into a universal principle'.[73]

The priest, then, makes a series of complicated, provocative and we might even say contradictory moves during his discourse. First, he appeals to the authority of the scriptures that preface the law. Then, after having castigated K for not 'having enough respect for the written word', he sets to work on a series of interpretations that implicitly must also be distinguished from the unalterable scripture. The contradiction can, of course, be explained by what we have already called a 'negative theology' of law. In this regard, the priest could be said to be mapping out the conditions of possibility for an immanent critique of his own discourse by making the law the thing beyond human judgement. In this sense, the transcendence of the law always has the power to wrestle one away from this or that judgement based on this or that interpretation. Here we could speak about the contradiction between the law and this or that interpretation as indicative or expressive of an irreducible distance or height at the heart of the transcendent. But how, then, do we explain the reconnection of the law to its representative in the form of the doorkeeper? The priest, let us remind ourselves, suggests that to pass judgement on the doorkeeper, to doubt the doorkeeper, is 'to doubt the Law itself'. This, Deleuze and Guattari would say, is where the demands of hidden transcendence, of religiosity, give way to that which 'constructs the law in the name of an immanent power of the one who enounces it'.[74] The 'one' constructing the law is, of course, the priest who concludes with the imperative that it is necessary to accept the law as law. The acceptance of the necessity of law, from a Deleuze-Guattarian perspective, is from first to last a political one. K's 'melancholy conclusion' does not even accord with his 'final judgement', yet he submits to it, or lets it impose itself on him. Kafka writes:

> K ... was too tired to survey all the conclusions arising from the story, and the trains of thought into which it was leading him were unfamiliar, dealing with impalpabilities better suited to a theme for discussion among Court officials than for him. The simple story had lost its clear outline, he wanted to put it out of his mind, and the priest, who now showed great delicacy of feeling, suffered him to do so and accepted his comment in silence, although undoubtedly he did not agree with it.[75]

Kafka's humour is again clearly in evidence here. Reading the passage in abstraction or isolation, we could be forgiven for thinking that the 'great delicacy of feeling' shown by the priest toward K is reflective of his humanity, benevolence even. But the tenor of the 'In the Cathedral' chapter directly and profoundly contradicts any such conclusion. We should note immediately that the priest accepts K's 'melancholy conclusion' – that is, 'It turns lying into a universal principle' – 'in silence, although undoubtedly he did not agree with it'. In other words, Kafka is showing that the priest has no further need to argue and engage with K, that he has effectively worn him down and succeeded in fatiguing him into submission. As Kafka says above: 'K ... was too tired to survey all the conclusions arising from the story and the trains of thought into which it was leading him were unfamiliar, dealing with impalpabilities better suited to a theme for discussion among Court officials than for him'. If this is a key sentence in this passage – or indeed key with respect to the chapter – then it is because it charts a movement whereby K's fatigue ('too tired') connects to a desire to submit to the power of the court (as the Court is thought to be 'better suited' to grappling with the 'impalpabilities' of the story and, by implication, K's own case). The induction of fatigue and political subjugation operates to the extent that the priest, as functionary of the Court, shapes K's desire, a desire to communicate his submission to the Court, which is expressed through his fatigued indifference as such. So it is in this sense that supposedly theological themes concerning the transcendence of the law give way to the politics of desire and, in this case, the power politics of subjugation.

By translating law into power, and subsequently translating or connecting power to desire, Kafka is not simply showing us the dangers inherent in any subjugation or submission to power as expressed through a given institutional or bureaucratic form. In other words, Kafka is not simply providing a commentary that cautions us not to invest too much power in the institutional or bureaucratic machine. Rather, by tracing 'the experiments on the functioning' of the bureaucratic or institutional machine that is the law, he makes possible or thinks a 'politics of desire' where the very concept of 'power' itself becomes problematized, where 'power' is thought differently as such. Making a distinct connection between Kafka and the work of their contemporary Michel Foucault, particularly the Foucault of *Discipline and Punish*, Deleuze and Guattari argue that Kafka's writing shows that power 'is not pyramidal as the Law would have us believe; it is segmentary and linear, and it proceeds by means of contiguity, and not by height ...'.[76] Thus, power is not something to be deferred to, submitted to, possessing a height and casting a long shadow on its subjects; power is not simply centralized and hierarchical, but is, on the contrary, something on the move, defined by its relations, by connections, by the way it cuts across certain neighbourhoods and borders, effecting 'deterritorializations'. Power, connected to the Deleuze-Guattarian notion of desire, becomes a connector itself, the expression of a connection; or it can testify to its blockage. We see glimpses of this power expressed through K's own movements throughout the 'In the Cathedral' chapter. For example, at an early point during their discussion the priest explicitly tells K that the verdict is likely to go against him, but K rallies somewhat by telling the priest of his readiness to enlist more help in his defence. 'There are several possibilities,' K tells the priest, 'I haven't explored yet.' 'You cast about too much for outside help,' retorts the priest disapprovingly, 'especially from women. Don't you see that it isn't the right kind of help?' Consider K's response:

> In some cases, even in many, I could agree with you ..., but not always. Women have great influence. If I could move some women I know to join forces in working for me, I couldn't help winning through. Especially before this Court, which consists entirely of petticoat hunters. Let the examining Magistrate see a woman in the distance and he almost knocks down his desk and the defendant in his eagerness to get at her.[77]

We immediately see that K's response is predicated on a clear connection between law, power and desire as expressed through his suggestion that the Court 'consists entirely of petticoat hunters', that the 'examining Magistrate' would almost knock down 'his desk and the defendant' to get at a woman. By connecting the power and procedures of the Court to a certain libidinal economy, by making the wheels of justice turn in a rather libidinous direction, K is in a sense potentially short-circuiting the power relations that are beginning to develop between him and the priest and, by extension, the Court. Against a 'negative theology' of law that would forever question K's assumptions about the status, scope and functioning of the law (thus leaving him fatigued and subjugated), K, at least in this fleeting but very important moment, thinks and asserts its 'desiring quality', or he asserts that 'Justice' is, in fact, 'desire'.[78] Coming back to Deleuze and Guattari's (Foucault-inspired) conception of power, then, we could say that Kafka is showing us that power need not simply be centralized and hierarchical, that it is not something simply possessed by some and lacking among others, but that it is *relational*, the product of a negotiation in which libidinal investments are key and where the political stakes are high. That the political stakes are high at this moment of negotiation between the K and the priest is shown by the way the priest responds to K. The priest responds with silence, he seems to understand that even though K exhibits a tendency to think Justice in connection to desire, to move and shift the power and process of Court proceedings in this explicitly libidinous direction, he also crucially understands that K has from the very beginning of their negotiation invested a certain 'trust' in him, that K is submissive and dependent on the judgements received from him as a functionary of the Court. Kafka describes the scene:

> 'Are you angry with me?' asked K of the priest. 'It may be that you don't know the nature of the Court you are serving'. He got no answer. 'These are only personal experiences' said K. There was still no answer from above. 'I wasn't trying to insult you' said K. And at that the priest shrieked from the pulpit: 'Can't you see anything at all?' It was an angry cry, but at the same time sounded like the involuntary shriek of one who sees another fall and is startled out of himself.[79]

K tries to make a connection, to facilitate a libidinous turn that would empower him to renegotiate the power relations in which he finds himself. This is itself an expression of power, power as expressed through making a connection (that is, connecting Justice to desire). Cutting across any assumed or received boundaries concerning law, power and desire or precipitating a kind of 'deter-ritorialization' of law, power and desire, becomes a possibility in 'In the Cathedral', even if this seemingly ends in failure. It would seem that K's tendency to deterritorialize law and power by connecting it to desire fails to go far enough precisely because his desire still importantly pivots around an investment in the priest as a figure of authority. This is evident from the above passage as K refuses to content himself regarding the substance of his own claims and constantly seeks reassurance from the priest. Unlike the priest's question which is caustic, accusatory and damning ('Can't you see anything at all?'), K's question is tentative, as he is scrab-bling for approval and seeking after a judgement ('Are you angry with me?'). The priest reasserts power here by aggressively refusing the libidinous turn suggested by K, and it is at this point that he really begins to work on him and on the idea that K has deluded himself as to the nature of the Court, a delusion he tries to illus-trate by way of the parable we outlined above. In one sense, this delicate and important moment of negotiation between K and the priest is the most expressly political moment precisely because the negotiation of power relations between them has not yet been fore-closed, the foreclosure comes in and through the parable itself, or as the parable takes hold and a 'negative theology' of law fatigues K into submission. If K is 'deluded' in the end, then this is because he is deluded with regard to the priest as a functionary of the Court, a man whose 'good intentions seemed to K beyond ques-tion'.[80]

Although we may again wonder whether Kafka is pulling our leg here, whether K's desire to submit himself to an authority figure (in this case, the priest) simultaneously expresses a *becoming molecular* of this figure, a figure comically exaggerated and rendered absurd. We should note that the priest imposes himself on K by shrieking from his inflated position in the pulpit. Are we not confronted with a rather comic or ridiculous image of the priest here? We should also note that the priest's accusatory and damning remark is an 'involuntary' one that startles him 'out of himself'. Do we not find ourselves confronted with an image of an authority figure that speaks by way of an indirect discourse, at the service of words that don't belong to him, words that condense social-political forces or a 'collective assemblage of enunciation' that functions to pattern the law or juridical machine as such? Even the most vaguely affirmative response to these questions necessitates that we emphasize that it is just too simple to say that the politics of desire or libidinal negotiation between K and priest in the cathedral ends in the priest's triumphant assertion of a 'negative theology' of law and in the subsequent subjugation of K. As has already been said, Deleuze and Guattari caution us to a 'careful' reading of *The Trial* and against any particularly tragic, fatalistic or humourless reading of what is a 'highly ambiguous' cathedral chapter. Tragic, fatalistic readings of *The Trial* inevitably point to the book's conclusion and to K's execution; but, and this is crucial from a Deleuze-Guattarian perspective, they ignore Kafka's humour, the comic exaggeration and critique of power and authority, the way figures of authority and power are politicized by being plugged into the social-political-economic-juridical forces that pulse through them and shape desire. Max Brod said that when Kafka read aloud passages of *The Trial* he and his listeners laughed uncontrollably, and we have seen that Deleuze and Guattari force us to take seriously this humourous sensibility.[81] Again we can go right back to the very first quote from *Kafka* used earlier in this chapter: 'Everything leads to laughter, starting with *The Trial*'.

I want to bring this part of the chapter (and indeed the chapter as a whole) to a conclusion by coming back to the claim with which it began. Earlier we suggested that if Kafka can be viewed as a realist, then this is a realism anchored not so much in a fidelity to the real as represented but rather through a form of writing and thinking that 'experiments' on the real, defamiliarizing it and making it take flight. And we have seen, more specifically, how Kafka does this in *The Trial* by the way his writing operates like a 'report of the experiments on the functioning of a machine' that gives shape and form to the law or Justice. So it is not simply that Kafka comments on the law, or denounces the law as unchecked or 'totalitarian' power. To be sure, *The Trial* can be read as commentary in this way; as, say, an exemplary cautionary tale against state power or bureaucratic and instrumental reason. But, from a Deleuze-Guattarian perspective, this is not the whole story for this simple reason that by experimenting on the real, a writer and thinker like Kafka is no longer simply commenting on the status and scope of things, re-presenting things to us, but is making things shift, move or take flight. Kafka does not simply re-present the thing we call law to us in narrative content, but follows a series of experiments whereby the law is itself thought to be plugged into an operating machine that connects it up to other things and, in so doing defamiliarizes it. We have seen how in *The Trial* law is connected to 'negative theology', connected to an image of scripturally sanctioned power, how this image of power is then connected to desire and the 'politics of desire' expressed through the negotiation of certain libidinal investments (for example, K and the priest in the cathedral) and where power itself then becomes thought and problematized along quasi Foucauldian lines (that is, power as relational and connective, the product of a negotiation in which libidinal investments are key, and where the political stakes are high).

And finally, a word on the notion of political critique that emerges from this image of Kafka experimenting on the real. As Deleuze and Guattari emphasize and demonstrate, Kafka confronts us with a critique of any image of critique grounded solely or simply in representation. From a social and political critique grounded in representation or commentary (for example, *The Trial* as a critical commentary on how the law works in proto-totalitarian societies or how it will work in the totalitarian societies to come if we are not careful) Kafka moves critique on; or, better still, his writing embodies and thinks a form of political critique as a kind of movement as such. Again this is the flight of defamiliarization or 'deterritorialization' expressed through the experimentation on the real as such. Earlier we noted that Deleuze and Guattari claimed that Kafka makes 'social representations' take flight precisely by connecting them to 'assemblages' which are then 'dismantled', a dismantling that expresses or thinks a 'deterritorialization of the world that is itself political'. And again this is what we experience in *The Trial*, or what we have seen more particularly in the cathedral chapter as any representation of law immediately gives way to a problematization of law through its connection to negative theology, which is then connected to scripturally sanctioned power, which is then connected to desire and the politics of desire, which is then set in motion by the negotiation of libidinal investments.

Key here, to repeat, is the movement itself, the making of connections and this, Deleuze and Guattari never tire of saying, is never merely a mediated commentary or representation of the 'political'. Put simply and directly, the politics and the political critique expressed and thought through a Kafka text such as *The Trial* is to be immediately found in the movement it charts, the connections it makes, the defamiliarizations it brings about.

# 2 • Painting

Deleuze and Guattari immediately force us to confront the idea that there is an ethics and politics always-already at play in painting. This, they suggest, is expressed in and through the way painting engages and thinks the 'face' or the 'abstract machine of faciality'. In order to make sense and render this intuition concrete it is important again to draw on Deleuze and Guattari's *A Thousand Plateaus*, in particular plateau seven, 'Year Zero: Faciality'.[1] This will be our focus in the second part of the chapter, and what will begin to emerge here are two images of the political, one the subject of a Deleuze-Guattarian critique, the other the object of ethical affirmation or, perhaps more accurately, ethico-political affirmation. What do I mean? On the one hand, Deleuze and Guattari insist that there is a politics of the face, that the face 'is a politics'. And by this they mean that the face (not just the images of the face that come to dominate the history of painting, but also what they call the processes of 'facialization' that are implied in and through all painting, whether figurative or not) is connected to a 'regime of signs', the political function of which is to reinforce 'majoritarian' norms or to sustain the kind of 'Power' that is assembled in what they call the 'state-form'. It is against this kind of politics that Deleuze and Guattari ethically and politically affirm the crucial importance of the forms of painting that 'deterritorialize' or 'dismantle' the face, and the painters who effect 'minoritarian' becomings that chart a movement beyond the 'representative threshold' of majoritarian norms and power. Simply put, to deterritorialize the face, to effect minoritarian becomings (these being the key functions of painting for Deleuze and Guattari), is always-already to think and actualize an ethics and a politics, an ethics and a politics of deterritorialization and minoritarian becoming.

So, what, we may ask, would such minoritarian becomings look like, or how are such becomings and deterritorializations actualized in and through the specific medium of painting? In the third and final part of the chapter we will look to Deleuze's specific engagement with Francis Bacon's work. And we will see that in *Francis Bacon* Deleuze gives us a very concrete feel for how Bacon's painting effects 'the deterritorialization of faces', and how his art actualizes or thinks minoritarian becomings which are at once ethical and political.[2] But before delving into Deleuze's *Francis Bacon* or indeed Deleuze and Guattari's *A Thousand Plateaus*, it will prove useful to dwell in the first part of the chapter on the concept of the 'face' found in the work of Emmanuel Levinas. Why this initial focus on Levinas when my express concern is with Deleuze and Guattari? The main impetus behind the intended juxtaposition of Levinasian and Deleuze-Guattarian images of the face is the creation of a montage, the effect of which will be to bring into focus a key aspect of Deleuze and Guattari's critical engagement with painting: namely, that it is a critical engagement which has a distinct ethical as well as political tenor. Therefore, and in spite of key and fundamental differences, we shall see emerge a kind of formal connection between Levinas and Deleuze-Guattari to the extent that they share a concern to ethico-politically disrupt what we could call a rather pernicious politics of the gaze, a politics of the gaze which functions to drown difference in what Deleuze and Guattari call 'waves of sameness'.[3]

## Levinas's Ethics of the Face

Let us turn firstly then to Levinas. As is well known, one of Levinas's key concerns in *Totality and Infinity* is to connect a concept of the face to the ethical, to stress the relation between ethics and the face. Section Three, Part B, of *Totality and Infinity* carries the sub-heading 'Ethics and the Face' and in it Levinas writes of the face of 'the other' as that which confronts the I, which disrupts its subjectivity and vision, which establishes the oddest and almost incomprehensible intersubjective relation grounded in 'speech' or 'language': a 'relation without relation' in Levinas's own utterly intentional paradoxical formulation. Bear with me here as I directly quote at length parts of the first few paragraphs of this section of the book:

> Inasmuch as the access to beings concerns vision, it dominates those beings, exercises a power over them. A thing is *given*, offers itself to me. In gaining access to it I maintain myself within the same.

The face is present in its refusal to be contained. In this sense it cannot be comprehended, that is, encompassed. It is neither seen nor touched – for in visual or tactile sensation the identity of the I envelops the alterity of the object, which becomes precisely a content.

The Other is not other with relative alterity ... The alterity of the Other does not depend on any quality that would distinguish him from me, for a distinction of this nature would precisely imply between us that community of genus which already nullifies alterity ...

The relation between the Other and me, which draws forth in his expression, issues neither in number or in concept. The Other remains infinitely transcendent, infinitely foreign; his face in which his epiphany is produced and which appeals to me breaks with the world that can be common to us ... Speech proceeds from absolute difference ...

Absolute difference ... is established only by language. Language accomplishes a relation between terms that breaks up the unity of a genus. The terms, the interlocutors, absolve themselves from the relation, or remain absolute within the relationship. Language is perhaps defined as the very power to break the continuity of being or of history ...

The fact that the face maintains a relation with me by discourse does not range him in the same; he remains absolute in the relation ... [T]he ethical relationship which subtends discourse ... puts the I in question. The putting in question emanates from the other.[4]

There are a number of points that are worth emphasizing or re-emphasizing in light of what Levinas is saying in this context. First, and most obviously, the relation to the other mediated through the face and accomplished in what he variously calls 'speech' 'language' or 'discourse' is an 'ethical relationship'. Second, the 'ethical relationship' so constituted is not a relationship we have in 'common' with each other, but a relation in which the face of the 'other' disrupts the I, where it 'puts the I in question'. This, third, is an important problematization of a tradition of thinking that trades on the politics of the gaze and the corresponding objectification of the other as gazed at. Of course, in one sense, Levinas would agree with the Sartre of *Being and Nothingness*,[5] with the Laura Mulvey of 'Visual Pleasure and Narrative Cinema',[6] with the John Berger of *Ways of Seeing*,[7] that visual access to beings (for example, the movie stars plastered across our cinema and TV screens, the female nudes plastered across our museum walls, the top-shelves of our corner-shops and, increasingly of course, of the web-sites 'we' seem to be accessing) implies a 'domination' of those beings, the exercise of 'power'. And yet, such is the provocation of Levinas, he refuses to rest content with an image of the face as objectification through gaze. He makes the face, or believes the face to be, its very own site of refusal, the face is in its very essence the 'refusal to be contained' within any politics of the gaze. The face as it is drawn forth in speech 'cuts across vision'.[8]

So the relation I have to the other mediated through the face and brought forth in discourse is a relation of disruption, an odd inter-subjective relation, a 'relation without relation' in Levinasian parlance. What does this mean? Or, putting the question a little more forcefully, perhaps, how can the idea of an intersubjective 'relation without relation' even begin to make any sense? For how can there be a relation between beings when the other remains, in the words of Levinas, 'infinitely transcendent', 'infinitely foreign'? How can interlocutors in discourse 'absolve themselves from the relation' or 'remain absolute within the relationship'? How can an intersubjective relation be logically maintained when any distinction between the I and the other cannot be identified, when the very identification of difference (for example, you and I are different, or we think that our relations with one another should be governed differently, or we think we should work out our differences in a respectful and tolerant way, in a way that respects each other's autonomy) already 'nullifies' difference, what Levinas above calls the 'alterity of the other'? A good way to navigate these questions is by drawing some help from the philosopher Simon Critchley whose writing is often defined by the energy and clarity with which it puts Levinasian concepts to work. For instance, in a recent work, *Infinitely Demanding*, Critchley tackles head-on Levinas's notion of the 'relation without relation', arguing that it is a key concept of *Totality and Infinity*. Consider, then, the following passages in which Critchley determines the core formal structure of Levinas's ethics of the face, clarifying at once the status and scope of the curious asymmetry of Levinasian intersubjectivity:

> In my view, the basic operation of Levinas's entire work is the experi-
> ence of an exorbitant demand which heteronomously determines the
> ethical subject ... I am not the equal of the demand that is made upon
> me. It is this fundamental inadequacy of approval to demand that

explains why ... the relation to the other is assymetrical. That is, the subject relates itself to something that exceeds it relational capacity. This is what Levinas paradoxically calls '*le rapport sans rapport*', the relation without relation, which is arguably the central concept of Levinas's *Totality and Infinity*. Yet, how can there be a relation between beings that remain absolute within that relation? Logically speaking, this is a contradiction in terms, yet it is precisely such a relation that Levinas wants to describe as ethical.

The difficulty can be illuminated by considering the function of the concept of infinity in Levinas's work. From the late 1950s onwards, he describes the ethical relation to the other in terms of infinity. What does this mean? ... The idea is that the ethical relation to the other has a *formal* resemblance to the relation, in Descartes's Third Meditation, between *res cogitans* and the infinity of God. What interests Levinas in this moment of Descartes's argument is that the human subject has an idea of infinity, and that this idea, by definition, is a thought that contains more than can be thought ...[9]

Critchley clarifies the status and scope of Levinasian intersubjectivity by reminding us of the importance of the concept of 'infinity', and the key sensibility here is one of overflow and paradox, of thought containing more (in Descartes's case 'God', in Levinas's case 'the other', in Critchley's case the demand that is the constitutive split at the heart of 'ethical subjectivity' or 'ethical experience'[10]) than can be thought. If this seems an odd or counter-intuitive idea of intersubjectivity, then from a Levinasian perspective it is perhaps important to interrogate why, precisely, we would feel that way? From a Levinasian point of view, it is crucial that we come to understand intersubjectivity, the ethical relation of the I to the other, is terms of what he calls 'heteronomy' rather than 'autonomy', and it is the rather problematic dominance of the concept of 'autonomy' that perhaps shapes our sense that Levinasian intersubjectivity is in some way counter-intuitive. What, then, is meant by 'autonomy' in this context, and how has it come to dominate our thinking in ethical-political matters? Here we must look to the importance and influence of Kant's work in the fields of ethics and politics, and to what Critchley calls the 'autonomy orthodoxy' that follows from this work.[11] As is well known, Kantian ethics and politics is grounded on a principle of 'autonomy', where the maxims upon which the subject acts are precisely those the subject gives to itself. The I is the source of the moral, and there can be no authority determined in moral deliberation without the free assent of the I. Morality, or ethics, presupposes the autonomy of the subject. And the subject remains in the bonds of unenlightened servitude for as long as moral norms or ethical values are imposed on it from the outside and for as long as the subject unthinkingly defers to the other or others outside itself. As Kant says in 'What is Enlightenment': 'If I have a book which understands for me, a pastor who has a conscience for me, a physician who decides my diet, ... I need not trouble myself. I need not think ... – others will readily undertake the irksome work for me'.[12]

So if 'enlightenment' for Kant presupposes a 'release' from 'self-incurred tutelage', and if this tutelage is reflected in our lack of will and courage to use our reason 'without direction from another' (say a figure of authority such as a 'pastor'), then clearly the heteronomy or otherness of this other is a threat to the development of autonomy. 'Have the courage', urges Kant, 'to use your own reason – that is the motto of the enlightenment'.[13] So there would seem to be a stark difference between Kantian and Levinasian ethics to the extent that the latter wants to think the ethical precisely as an experience of 'heteronomy', the former seeing 'heteronomy' as a possible threat to the subject's freedom. Of course, this does not mean that Levinas simply wants to invert Kantian premises by somehow arguing that an ethics follows from the simple internalization or unthinking acceptance of moral norms imposed heteronomously on the subject. Put simply, Levinas does not want to deny the importance of what Kant would call autonomy or freedom, but rather he wants to affirm the primacy of a certain notion of heteronomy and to understand the latter as that which conditions the former. The 'ethical relationship' to the other is first and foremost heteronomous; the other is irreducible, 'infinitely foreign', 'infinitely transcendent', and the demands it places on the subject, mediated through the face and brought forth in 'language', call the subject 'into question'. So before autonomy, before the activity of the thinking subject, there is heteronomy, the otherness that infinitely conditions my thinking about matters of morality and infinitely calls this thinking into question. We cannot from a Levinasian perspective take cognizance of the other's autonomy or collectively reflect it in our actions precisely because our cognizance or very cognitive powers in confronting the other confront the infinite itself. Our desire to fashion or conceptualize an image of the other after the self, or in conjunction with an inter-subjective self, can forever be thwarted by the act of the other's refusal (remembering from the passage initially quoted above that the other presents itself 'in its refusal to be contained', it 'cannot be comprehended, that is encompassed'). In this sense, the infinity of the other takes on a concrete form by way of a particular act of refusal that is, in principle, eternal or without end.[14]

Following Maurice Blanchot, Critchley emphasizes Levinas's idea that the ethical relation to the other mediated through the face and drawn forth in language produces a 'curvature of intersubjec-tive space'. This is an interesting image, and I think it captures well the provocation of Levinas's thinking or conception of intersubjec-tivity. When Levinas speaks, as he does in his conclusions to *Totality and Infinity*, of this 'curvature of intersubjective space' he tends to image it as a confrontation with height. The other 'comes from on high' and the 'curvature of intersubjective space inflects distance into elevation'.[15] What does this mean? It means that when I confront the other I experience the other as the high point of the curvature, all that I can have is a low-angle shot of the other. Put another way, the notion of a third-person perspective on the ethical relation is impossible as a God-like or third eye view (that is, the over-head shot that impassively surveys the terrain or 'subjective field' as Levinas calls it) is impossible without totalizing and nullifying the 'absolute difference' of the relation. As a phenomenologist Levinas is wholly committed to the immanence of the relation, to what is actually going on in and through the relation as experienced and the experience for him, of course, is that of the heteronomy of the other's demand that places the I in question. So, one of the provocative consequences of the Levinasian conception of intersubjectivity can be made clear; namely, that any dialogical model of intersubjectivity becomes problematic to the extent that it ends in abstraction, a technical camera eye suppos-edly removed from the relation but, in truth, framing the relation from the very first instance. We could briefly consider, for example, the hugely influential concept of intersubjectivity that is at play in Habermas's ethics and politics.[16] As is well known, Habermas, like Kant, is concerned with the autonomy of the subject, and he is concerned to locate this autonomy in the intersubjective relation – this is what he famously calls 'communicative action oriented to mutual understanding'. Habermas's basic point is that autonomy, and indeed social reciprocity and equality, is built into the very structure of our intersubjective and communicative relations. The freedom of the subject can only be recognized and realized through a form of communicative action in which the individual right to assert autonomy in the first person is universally and reciprocally guaranteed. Put yet another way, the autonomy of the subject, and the communicative relations or 'communication community' in which this autonomy is asserted, form an inextricable link in the formation of the 'intersubjective core of the self'.[17] Of course, the problem here, at least from a Levinasian perspective, is that a dialogical or communicative model such as Habermas's only appears to be offering the possibility of a self-other relation grounded in autonomy, equality/reciprocity if we accept it as a neutral, third-person perspective that somehow stands outside the relation. Levinas's polemical point being that such supposedly impassive neutral seeing or 'vision' is 'deformed' in the 'curvature of intersubjective space' and any supposedly neutral or impartial conception of the self-other relation remains unresponsive to the otherness of the other, or what he also calls 'exteriority'.[18]

## The Face and Deleuze-Guattari

You may be forgiven for wondering why I have spent this time on Levinas's ethics of the face, especially when my express concern here is with Deleuze and Guattari's concept of painting, and the politics of painting. As I stated at the beginning of the chapter, the main impetus behind the intended juxtaposition of Levinasian and Deleuze-Guattarian images of the face is the creation of a montage, the cross-cutting effect of which will be to bring into focus a key aspect of Deleuze and Guattari's critical engagement with painting: namely, that it is a critical engagement that has a distinct ethical as well as political tenor. Therefore, and in spite of key and fundamental differences, we shall see emerge a kind of formal connection between Levinas and Deleuze-Guattari to the extent that they share a concern ethico-politically to disrupt a rather pernicious politics of the gaze; a politics of the gaze that functions to drown difference in (to repeat Deleuze and Guattari's rather Levinasian terminology) 'waves of sameness'.

Of course, before we can even begin to make sense of the idea that the Deleuze-Guattarian image of the face is in some way formally connected to a Levinasian conception, we need to be clear about the concept in question. What precisely do Deleuze and Guattari mean with they talk about the face or faciality? More particularly, what do they mean what they say 'the face is a politics'?[19] Well, one thing that could be said is that the face implies recognition – a politics of recognition, although it is important to point out that we are very far away from the kind of 'politics of recognition' made famous by, say, Charles Taylor. As is well known, Taylor's politics of recognition is tied inextricably to a 'multi-culturalist' discourse of tolerance and respect, where the 'difference' of other cultures deserve respect on the basis that they, as Taylor says, 'have provided a horizon of meaning for large numbers of human beings … over a long period of time' and that 'it would take supreme arrogance to discount this'.[20] Simply put, this kind of politics of recognition, inflected with this idea of a multicultural sensibility, has a clear moral or ethical sense for Taylor, and failure to adopt this multicultural sensibility is – and Taylor is explicit on this – a 'moral failing', reflecting the 'supreme arrogance' of those ethnocentrically immured by their own cultural norms and values.[21] From a Deleuze-Guattarian perspective, the notion of a 'politics of recognition' only really makes sense *as a politics*, and as a potentially more pernicious and darker politics to boot. There is what they call an 'abstract machine of faciality' that proceeds by way of recognition, but recognition here functions on the basis of a regime that sifts and sorts, that normalizes and rejects, that forces a certain conformity to the majoritarian norm, that tends, even, towards 'racism'. As Deleuze and Guattari argue:

> [T]he abstract machine of faciality assumes a role of selective response, or choice: given a concrete face, the machine judges whether it passes or not, whether it goes or not … At every moment, the machine rejects faces that do not conform, or seem suspicious … [Y]ou've been recognized, the abstract machine has you inscribed in its overall grid. It is clear that in its … role as deviance detector, the faciality machine does not restrict itself to individual cases but operates [as] the computation of normalities. If the face is in fact … your average ordinary White Man, then the first deviances … are racial: yellow man, black man …

Racism operates by the determination of degrees of deviance in relation to the White-Man face...From the viewpoint of racism, there is no exterior, there are no people on the outside. There are only people who should be like us and whose crime is not to be ... Racism never detects the ... other; it propagates waves of sameness until those who resist identification have been wiped out (or those who only allow themselves to be identified at a given degree of divergence). Its cruelty is equaled only by its incompetence and naiveté.[22]

The contrast between Deleuze-Guattari and Taylor here is striking. For Taylor, multiculturalism and a tolerance of the other is key to militating against the immorality or racism that can follow from being ethnocentrically immured by one's own cultural values, and it is crucial to a politics of recognition that 'we' approach the other outside our own cultural framework and dialogically engage them through the development of what Taylor would call a 'language of perspicuous contrast'; that is, a conversation that is disruptive of mono-cultural identity.[23] For Deleuze and Guattari, contra Taylor, it is never a question of bemoaning a lack of a multicultural sensibility, a lack of dialogue, a lack of any kind of 'language of perspicuous contrast', or even understanding 'racism' as a politics of exclusion, 'the designation of someone as other'.[24] When Deleuze and Guattari say that racism 'operates by the determination of degrees of deviance in relation to the White-Man face', that it implies 'no exterior' or 'no people on the outside' and 'propagates waves of sameness until those who resist identification have been wiped out', they implicitly and explicitly challenge any dialogical model of the other or, more specifically, any kind of liberal-multicultural sensibility that would seem to desire the inclusion of the other within an image of the same (in the case of Taylor, a dialogue of 'perspicuous contrast' in which ethnocentrically formed identities are disrupted and reformed in light of the emergence of a new dialogical subject or 'we'). Indeed, and pressing the point further still, a liberal-multicultural desire to range in the other within a regime of 'sameness' would seem to have the precise formal structure of 'racism'. Such is the provocation of Deleuze and Guattari's approach to the politics of recognition as it is effected through the 'abstract machine of faciality'.

Another key difference here is that Deleuze and Guattari are discussing the problematic of 'racism' in terms that are not simply reducible to a problem of language. It is not simply the case that Deleuze and Guattari would believe that we lack a language (Taylorian dialogue, Habermasian communication or whatever) to critically challenge power and prejudice, but that it is not a purely linguistic matter. Of course, and as we have seen in chapter one, Deleuze and Guattari offer us a pragmatics that is acutely sensitive to the ways in which our social and political world is shaped by language, and the importance of language and indeed literature in thinking the political is something they affirm constantly. The point here is that the face, the 'abstract machine of faciality', is crucially a visual thing, it poses a problem of the visual, hence the connection of the concept of faciality to an expressly visual medium such as painting. Thus when Deleuze and Guattari speak about the face, or the abstract machine of faciality, in connection to a 'regime of signs' that can produce, sift and shape subjectivities (that is, 'woman', 'yellow man', 'black man') on a sliding scale of conformity to a majoritarian norm (that is, 'white man') they are seeking to analyse this 'regime of signs' in visual terms. So what, then, is the relation between a visual medium such as painting and a given regime of signs? Importantly, it is never simply a question of the regime of signs reflecting or re-presenting and indeed demanding conformity with a majoritarian norm. There is, as Deleuze and Guattari say, a 'brighter side' to the extent that painting has often explored the possibility of taking the majoritarian face (the 'Christ-face' as they also call it) in all manner of other directions, the possibility of opening up the majoritarian face to all manner of minoritarian becomings (Christ becoming 'queer' or 'negro').[25] Here we confront what is the key function of painting for Deleuze and Guattari; namely, *painting as a deterritorialization of the face*. And if the 'aim of painting has always been the deterritorialization of faces',[26] and if the face 'is a politics' precisely by being connected to a 'regime of signs' that can produce, sift and shape subjectivities on a sliding scale of conformity to a majoritarian norm, then painting immediately is a visual form that thinks and can effect minoritarian becomings that are, in their own way, political; that is, political by way of the movements they chart and the differences they make to the given regime of signs.

What would such minoritarian becomings look like? And how are such becomings actualized by way of the specific medium of painting? As has already been indicated, in order to address these key questions directly it will be important for us to consider Deleuze's particular engagement with Francis Bacon's work, for in *Francis Bacon* Deleuze gives us a very concrete feel for how Bacon's painting effects 'the deterritorialization of faces', how his art thinks or actualizes minoritarian becomings (in particular what he would call 'becoming-animal'). For the moment, though, this discussion of Deleuze's Bacon will be postponed in order to maintain a focus on how a juxtaposition of Levinasian and Deleuze-Guattarian concepts of the face may bring into view a kind of formal homology or connection between them. What do I mean here?

Well, as has already been noted, Deleuze and Guattari juxtapose their image of the faciality machine (with its majoritarian gaze detecting deviance on a sliding slide, with the propagation of 'waves of sameness', the identification of the other as the same, the wiping out of the other as such) with the 'brighter side' of deterritorialization and minoritarian becoming. So there is a politics of a majoritarian gaze and a counter politics of deterritorialization and minoritarian becoming. And, at a certain level of formal abstraction, I think we can begin to see some connections with Levinas here. Like Deleuze and Guattari, Levinas equally wants to resist the propagation of 'waves of sameness' or any identification of the other within a given regime of the same. As with Deleuze and Guattari, Levinas forces us to interrogate, indeed to critique, any ethics and politics grounded in what we have been calling a dialogical model of the other. As was seen earlier, Levinas's model of intersubjectivity remains provocative and retains a particular polemical force against, for example, a Habermasian conception of intersubjectivity grounded in the possibility of equality and social reciprocity. At its most provocative, Levinasian ethics is precisely concerned to caution against such a model by understanding it in terms of a regime of the same, where the other is captured by a 'vision' of the self-other relation that is supposedly passive and neutral, but which, in truth, operates in order to frame the other in conjunction with the 'I'; the politics of making the other more like me. And we have seen that Levinas insists that in the 'curvature of intersubjective space' such supposedly impassive, neutral seeing or 'vision' is 'deformed' in the concrete gesture of the other's refusal to be reined in with regard to the order of the same. Of course, for Deleuze and Guattari, the politics of making the other more like me or us is a form of 'racism'; a rather pernicious 'politics of recognition' that stands in extreme opposition to the kind of liberal-multiculturalist (and again thoroughly dialogical) model offered up in, for instance, the influential work of Charles Taylor. So, at a particular formal level, we have a connection between a Levinasian and Deleuze-Guattarian provocation, a polemic against a dialogical model of politics, a cautioning against the politics of making the other identify itself within a given regime of sameness.[27]

By referring to the kind of politics that surfs on the back of 'waves of sameness' as a form of 'cruelty', Deleuze and Guattari leave the reader in no doubt as to the tenor of their critique. The majoritarian gaze of the faciality machine is, in an important sense, intolerable to them. In this respect, their critique of this gaze has a clear resonance with the Levinasian gesture of ethico-politically disrupting the politics of the gaze. But what kind of ethico-political disruption are we talking about here? Or, to pose the question more directly perhaps, what kind of ethics is implied by Deleuze and Guattari's critique of the majoritarian gaze? I will make two gestures in response to this question. First, I would like further to explore the logic or binary of majoritarian-minoritarian that is crucial to Deleuze and Guattari's approach to the political, to their logic or ontology of the political.[28] Second, I want to show how this Deleuze-Guattarian political ontology of the majoritarian-minoritarian implies at once an ethics – an *ethics of autonomy* – that can be amplified a little by turning very briefly to Deleuze's work on Henri Bergson, in particular his early book *Bergsonism*.[29]

In a way, we can think of Deleuze and Guattari's ontology of the political as an ontology of tendencies and movements, tendencies and movements that thought, in its representationalist mode, momentarily suspends and captures within a given language or signifying apparatus (I will return to this important point shortly). As we have seen, Deleuze and Guattari use the language or binary of majoritarian-minoritarian in essaying a politics of the gaze as effected through the faciality machine and a counter-politics of becoming in and through which the former is deterritorialized. But how precisely do Deleuze and Guattari distinguish the majoritarian and minoritarian from one another? Consider the following passage, which is vintage Deleuze and Guattari and is well worth quoting at length:

The notion of *minority* is very complex, with musical, literary, linguistic, as well as juridical and political, references. The opposition between minority and majority is not simply quantitative. Majority implies a constant ..., serving as a standard measure by which to evaluate it ... It is obvious that 'man' holds the majority, even if he is less numerous than mosquitoes, children, women, blacks, peasants, homosexuals ... That is because he appears twice, once is the constant and again in the variable from which the constant is extracted. Majority assumes a state power and domination, not the other way around ... A determination different from that of the constant will therefore be considered minoritarian, by nature and regardless of number ... This is evident in all the operations, electoral or otherwise, where you are given a choice, but on condition that your choice conform to the limits of the constant ('you mustn't choose to change society ...'). But at this point, everything is reversed. For the majority, insofar as it is analytically included in the abstract standard, is never anybody, ... whereas the minority is the becoming of everybody, one's potential becoming to the extent that one deviates from the model. There is a majoritarian 'fact', but it is the analytic fact of Nobody, as opposed to the becoming-minoritarian of everybody. This is why we must distinguish between: the majoritarian as a constant and homogeneous system; minorities as subsystems; and the minoritarian as a potential, creative and created, becoming ... There is a universal figure of minoritarian consciousness as the becoming of everybody, and that becoming is creation ... The figure to which we are referring is continuous variation, as an amplitude that continually oversteps the representative threshold of the majoritarian standard ... In erecting the figure of a universal minoritarian consciousness, one addresses powers of becoming that belong to a different realm from that of Power and Domination. Continuous variation constitutes the becoming-minoritarian of everybody, as opposed to the majoritarian Fact of Nobody. Becoming minoritarian ... is called autonomy.[30]

This passage gives us a most concrete feel for how Deleuze and Guattari construct an argument and on what basis their thought proceeds. The key target here, as I hinted above, is a certain notion of representation. And Deleuze and Guattari's key strategy in this passage is literally to write against representation by repeatedly confronting us with a number of statements or, what they would call, 'slogans'. As was seen in the previous chapter, Deleuze and

Guattari offer us a pragmatics and politics of the slogan as opposed to a politics of representation, and in the above passage this distinction is clearly operating. Remember that for Deleuze and Guattari, language (or any signifying system) has a purely expressive power and capacity to intervene immediately in the social-political body, instantaneously and directly to change things – such is the singular effect of the slogan. So, what singular effect does the above passage have on our thinking with regard to the concepts 'majority' and 'minority', and how is this connected to a critique of the politics of representation?

Most immediately, we see there is a politics of representation implied in and through the majoritarian, where the 'majoritarian' implies a representation of a certain constant or standard (again we could think of the 'Christ-face' here, or what Deleuze and Guattari more generally refer to as 'the average adult-white-heterosexual-European-male speaking a standard language'). And this representative standard or 'representative threshold' is constantly crossed by minoritarian becomings, or the minoritarian is precisely the movement or becoming that charts a particular and critical deviation from the model. It is in this sense that we can begin to think the concepts of majority and minority in qualitative terms, that is, as tendencies and movements that traverse social and political life rather than as identifiable or quantifiable features or figures in social and political life. For instance, against the normative idea of a representative democracy in which the state ought to reflect or literally re-present numerically significant majority interests, where ideally some sense of collective will should inform majoritarian norms, Deleuze and Guattari provoca-tively suggest that majoritarian norms already have an in-built tendency to assume a state-form or 'state power and domination'. So before representation, or before the politics of representative democracy, we have a state-form or assemblage of power already in place. Before we choose our representatives, before we choose the representatives who share our norms and values, we already have a state-form or assemblage of power that demands a partic-ular kind of conformity to the 'limits of the constant'. 'Majority', then, is not the name for an identifiable or quantifiable thing or figure; it is a tendency in the political, a tendency towards power in the state-form. 'Minority', then, is not the numerically less signifi-cant (taken together there are more 'mosquitoes, children, women, blacks, peasants, homosexuals' than there are 'adult-white-heterosexual-European-males'), but a tendency to determine a 'difference' that deviates from that which is modeled on the power of the state-form.

From a Deleuze-Guattarian perspective, the concept of majority carries negative connotations, ontologically and politically. The majority is a negative figure, or more accurately is not a figure at all – it is 'the analytic fact of Nobody'. So the state-form or state power, on a strict Deleuze-Guattarian reading, belongs to a 'majority' that is a 'Nobody'; state power represents no one as power in the state-form is an abstraction that, in an important sense, remains unconnected to those of us who make up the body politic. Of course, it is very tempting to view what Deleuze and Guattari are saying here through some form of anarchist lens – although it is important to acknowledge that such a temptation carries some risk.[31] Is it productive to claim for Deleuze and Guattari a quasi-anarchist desire to disrupt the state-form, where the 'state-form' is inevitably viewed as that which remains abstracted from the body politic? I would suggest, following Todd May after a fashion, that there is a quasi-anarchism affirmed by Deleuze and Guattari when they pointedly counter pose the representation of the majoritarian 'Nobody' to the 'becoming-minoritarian of everybody', further connecting this idea of minoritarian becoming to a certain image or logic of autonomy, where 'autonomy' is expressly thought to be that which differs from the state-form.[32] A cross-comparison with Levinas is again possible in this regard. As Critchley shows, Levinas can be seen to provide us with a political or what he calls 'metapolitical' concept of anarchy, where 'anarchy' brings to mind an experience of the disturbance of the state-form, a state-form that functions in abstraction, at a certain distance from those who are subject to its power, and where, inevitably, that very distance becomes the source of another kind of power to be exercised by those subjects who can, as the state's other, question its authority as a totality, or question its ability to speak for the whole, for all of 'us'.[33]

Again, however, it is necessary to understand this quick cross-referencing of Levinas and Deleuze-Guattari in rather formal terms, or as a general observation that is inevitably complicated and rendered problematic as soon as the focus shifts to specific differences between them. Clearly, and as we have seen, Levinas would not want to use the language of 'autonomy' employed by Deleuze and Guattari. Further, Deleuze and Guattari would not be content to think about the critique and disturbance of the state-form as a 'moment of negation *without any* affirmation', which is precisely how Levinas defines 'anarchy' in *Otherwise than Being*.[34] Contra Levinas, then, Deleuze and Guattari insist on the importance of autonomy, and they would insist on the intuition that autonomy is expressed affirmatively; that is, autonomy emerges only as an act of creation, or in a moment of 'creative and created, becoming'. It is here that our discussion can most productively take the brief Bergsonian turn that I hinted at above. That is to say, the concept of autonomy at play in Deleuze-Guattari's political ontology of minoritarian becoming, their ethical affirmation of minoritarian becoming as autonomy, can be amplified and given further sense by referring back to Deleuze's earlier work, *Bergsonism*. In *Bergsonism*, Deleuze stresses the significance of a Bergsonian conception of freedom, where 'freedom' is expressed and affirmed by posing or constituting problems. It is through formulating, positing or inventing problems that freedom is affirmed. The constitution of a problem is always-already an affirmative act precisely because it is invention as such, precisely because it is a creative act as such. Drawing explicitly in detail and on quotes from Bergson's *Creative Evolution*, Deleuze writes:

> We are wrong to believe that the true and the false can only be brought to bear on solutions, that they only begin with solutions. This prejudice is social (for society, and the language that transmits its order-words, 'set up' ready-made problems, as if they were drawn out of the 'city's administrative filing cabinets', and force us to 'solve' them, leaving us only a thin margin of freedom). Moreover, this prejudice goes back to childhood, to the classroom: it is the schoolteacher who 'poses' the problems; the pupil's task is to discover the solutions. In this way we are kept in a kind of slavery. True freedom lies in the power to decide, to constitute problems themselves.[35]

The key to this passage as I want to read it here is the immediate and unselfconscious connection Deleuze makes between freedom and creation; the act of constituting something different, the emergence of something new. There is in Deleuze an ethics of autonomy or freedom, and freedom is affirmed in creation. Of course, all of this is well known, and the significant influence of Bergson on Deleuze and on Deleuze and Guattari's philosophy and ethics has rightly been widely acknowledged.[36] For us, though, the crucial point is that we connect back to the problem of painting. Or, to pose the question more directly: how can our discussion thus far concerning the Deleuze-Guattarian and Levinasian concepts of the face connect to Deleuze's analysis of Francis Bacon's work? As I have stressed, a focus on Levinas is useful in sensitizing us to the importance of the ethical in discussions of the face, or of the visual more generally. And mapped against the backdrop of Levinas, Deleuze and Guattari's concept of the face can be seen to have some formal connection to the former, at least in the sense that Deleuze and Guattari are also concerned ethically to question and interrogate any politics of the visual that pivots around a regime of the same. Of course, Deleuze and Guattari are not praising the heteronomy of the other; they are advocating an ethics and a politics of becoming-other, and this, against Levinas, is an ethics and politics of autonomy.

Turning finally to Deleuze's work on Bacon, it becomes important to preface it with the idea that the politics of deterritorialization (of the face) practised by Bacon is, in Deleuze's terms, always-already ethical; that ethics and politics coexist and are expressed through Bacon's painting to the extent that the latter effects a becoming-other as such. Nothing could be further from a Deleuzian engagement with Bacon than the idea of the latter as some kind of amoral, joyless and nihilistic artist. Rather than being content with the well-worn cliché that Bacon is, as John Berger puts it, a 'prophet of a pitiless world',[37] Deleuze rather interestingly sees him as a religious painter, or sees his paintings as forging connections with all that is radical and scandalously permissible in the 'religious' paintings of, say, Giotto or Tintoretto.[38] The key thing is that Bacon's work only becomes a cliché if we rest content with the cliché of the ready-made image of the painter and the painting. And crucially, for Deleuze, this is the very thing that Bacon's art thinks against; Bacon's painting, in other words, becomes an engagement with the cliché, or it becomes, it enters into becomings, to the degree that it problematizes the clichés and ready-made images that play through a world that tends to range us into the same.

## Bacon, Cliché and Becoming-animal

What precisely, then, is a cliché? For Deleuze, it is a prepictorial given, the 'painting before painting' as he calls it, a ready-made image or series of images. 'It is a mistake', Deleuze writes:

> to think that the painter works on a white surface … The painter has many things in his head, or around him, or in his studio. Now everything he has in his head or around him is already on the canvas, more or less virtually, more or less actually, before he begins his work. They are all present in the canvas as so many images, actual or virtual, so that the painter does not have to cover a blank surface, but rather would have to empty it out, clear it, clean it … In short, what we have to define are all these 'givens' that are on the canvas before the painter's work begins, and determine, among these givens, which are an obstacle, which are a help, or even the effects of a preparatory task.[39]

It is interesting to note that in this passage we have a condemnation of cliché and an acknowledgement that it may be a help, or even the possibility that the preparatory tasks the painter performs become inevitably entangled in cliché. Indeed, in the very next sentence Deleuze goes even further in explicitly saying that prepictorial givens, or 'figurative givens' are a 'prerequisite of painting'. So if the painter is besieged by figurative givens (that is, by 'photographs that are illustrations, by newspapers that are narrations, by cinema-images, by television images', by 'ready-made perceptions, memories, phantasms'[40]), then it is never a simple question of conquering them head-on, for a direct assault is itself far from unproblematic. If an artist 'is content to transform the cliché, to deform it or mutilate it, to manipulate it in every possible way, this reaction', Deleuze contends, is 'too intellectual: it allows the cliché to rise again from the ashes', it leaves us 'within the milieu of the cliché, or else it gives … no other consolation than parody'.[41] It is hard not to think of the work of David Lynch here, and the way in which he piles clichés of various sorts on top of one another. One could, for example, think of his television work, the cliché of the cliffhanger in *Twin Peaks*, where, in the finale to series one, he and Mark Frost packed fourteen different cliffhangers into this one particular episode. Or when, in a dream, the dead Laura Palmer reveals the identity of her killer to Agent Cooper at the end of one episode (we, the viewers, of course, don't hear what she says – hence the cliffhanger), Agent Cooper then completely forgets what she has told him by the beginning of the next episode.[42] In this sense, Lynch manipulates, indeed mutilates, the cliché – he effects a reflexive foregrounding of the cliché, parodies it and emphasizes its constitutive role in shaping the meanings we invest in the world around us. From a Deleuzian perspective, there is something interesting in almost suffocating the viewer in clichés, as a degree of abandon with regard to the cliché is required as a preparatory task for the artist. But, in the end, the artist must not rest content with a reflexive and parodic foregrounding of the cliché; in the end, there must be a rejection of the cliché, and only then 'can the work begin'.[43]

So what is to be done? How can the work begin? More particularly, in what sense can a painter like Bacon challenge the clichés and ready-made images that play through the canvas of our world, shaping it from the beginning? Deleuze emphasizes the importance of the free or 'manual marks' that Bacon makes on his canvas:

> the painter himself must enter into the canvas before beginning ... In this way, he enters into the cliché ... He enters into it precisely because he *knows what he wants to do*, but what saves him is the fact that he *does not know how to get there*, he does not know how to do what he wants to do. He will only get there by getting out of the canvas. The painter's problem is not how to enter into the canvas, since he is already there ..., but how to get out if it, thereby getting out of the cliché ... It is the chance manual marks that will give him the chance, though not a certitude ...[44]

As is well known, Bacon often used the tactic of making what he variously calls free, involuntary or 'irrational marks'. These marks function by chance, by accident, and in this sense they are 'non-representative'; they work against the re-presentation of the cliché; they work against the sameness of the ready-made image. How? 'These marks,' says Deleuze, 'can be called "non-representative" precisely because they depend on an act of chance and express nothing regarding the visual image ... In themselves they serve no other purpose than to be utilized and reutilized by the hand of the painter.'[45] We can consider, for example, Bacon's own account of the preparation and execution of his 1946 work *Painting*. Here we are confronted with a figure; perhaps a man, perhaps in a suit, perhaps sitting. The figure is positioned beneath various cuts of butcher meat, the upper half of the head is shadowed under an umbrella, the bottom half reveals a toothy grimace or grin (or a grin becoming a grimace, a grimace becoming a grin). Bacon's own account of creating this image in his now famous conversations with David Sylvester in *Interviews with Francis Bacon* is worth quoting here:

> FB Well one of the pictures I did in 1946 ... came to me as an accident. I was attempting to make a bird alighting on a field. And ... suddenly the lines that I'd drawn suggested something totally different, and out of this suggestion arose the picture. I had no intention to do this picture; I never thought of it that way. It was like one continuous accident mounting on top of another.
>
> DS Did the bird alighting suggest the umbrella or what?
>
> FB It suddenly suggested an opening-up into another area of feeling altogether. And then I made these things, I gradually made them. So ... I don't think the bird suggested the umbrella; it suddenly suggested the whole image. And I carried it out very quickly, in about three or four days.[46]

As we can begin to see, Bacon tends to think of the involuntary or non-rational marks as expressing a particular form of liberation of the painter's hand from the eye, where the eye narrates, organizes or re-presents a story and where the hand becomes a part of a developing image that breaks with the preconceived narrative, growing spontaneously and immanently, where the developing image seems to permit, as Deleuze says, 'the emergence of another world'.[47] In the case of *Painting*, the non-rational or 'non-representative' free marks are given through the drawing of lines, lines originally conceived in Bacon's mind's eye as 'a bird alighting on a field' but which become something other, another image. And, as Bacon emphasizes, it is not simply a matter of bird becoming an umbrella, but the marks or lines suggesting a 'whole image'; the accident, and the continuous piling up of accidents, in other words, has a form of autonomy, or is part of an immanently constitutive or self-forming activity in the first instance. In this way, Bacon is always looking to utilize and reutilize chance or accidents; for example, the swipe of the brush, the rag, the sponge, spillages, splatters, or even throwing paint. When pushed particularly by Sylvester as to why he may throw paint at a developing image, Bacon characteristically responds: 'I can only hope that the throwing of the paint onto the already made image or half-image will either re-form the image or that I will be able to manipulate this paint further ...'.[48]

So, by chance, by using chance and accident, nascent clichés buried in the mind's eye of the painter can be disrupted. And yet immediately the painter is faced, as Deleuze emphasizes, with the difficulty of not becoming mired in cliché, in a cliché of chance and accident itself. And key here, from a Deleuzian perspective, is the acknowledgement that Bacon always submits chance to function, to a particular use. Chance is, as Deleuze points out, always 'manipulated' chance for Bacon.[49] In a way we could think of Bacon's notion of manipulated chance as an important, even pre-emptive, response to one possible clichéd response to any art form that expresses or seeks to foreground chance as such. We can imagine a clichéd and caustic response such as: 'yes, yes, we understand this artwork as chance or accident, but so what, couldn't my three-year-old daughter do this'? Interestingly, an objection of this kind is explicitly put to Bacon by Sylvester. Referring, at one point, to Duchamp's 1913–14 work *Three Standard Stoppages* (a work in which he took three threads a metre length and dropped them from a height of a metre onto a painted canvas, then fixed them where they had fallen), Sylvester suggests that effectively anyone could have dropped the threads, perhaps his cleaner. Turning directly, then, to Bacon, he poses the question: 'could you ask your cleaner to come in, take a handful of paint, and at a certain moment, chosen by you, throw it at the canvas? Is it conceivable that she might get some useful results?' Bacon concedes the point that someone else could come into his studio throw paint on a canvas and 'create another image altogether or a better image'. But then he adds the following qualification:

> I would loathe my paintings to look like chancy abstract expressionist paintings, because I really like highly disciplined painting, although I don't use highly disciplined methods of constructing it. I think the only thing is that my paint looks immediate. Perhaps it's vanity to say that, but at least I sometimes think, in the better things, the paint has an immediacy, although I don't think it looks like thrown-about paint.[50]

For Bacon there is a tendency toward sloppiness in 'chancy abstract expressionist paintings', a lack of discipline, discipline that is needed to render the painting or image 'immediate'. And discipline here means 'manipulated', even controlled, chance. So, for example, the throwing of paint is controlled, to a degree at least, subject to a moment of decision as to when to throw; to judgments about the colour and consistency of the paint; to a specific region of the image at which the throw is aimed; to a sense of the force of the throw or the angle of the throw, which implies, of course, a practice and an experiential sense of what is likely to happen when the paint is thrown at a certain pace and from a particular angle. So how, we may ask, does this manipulation of chance render the image 'immediate'? Bacon's response is simple: the medium itself is a 'supple' medium, 'paint is so malleable that you never do really know'.[51] In other words, the immediacy is expressed through the malleability of the medium; paint is always-already chance and no matter how wilfully or intentionally it is put on a canvas it still is, as a medium, an immanently constitutive or self-forming form that needs to be expressed directly by way of the creation of immanently constitutive or self-forming images. 'I mean,' Bacon says, 'you even don't know that when you put it on wilfully, as it were, with a brush – you never quite know how it will go on.'[52]

Coming back explicitly to Deleuze in a summary fashion we can say that Bacon's challenge and engagement with cliché, with 'figurative givens', or with 'figuration' more generally, functions through a particular kind of labour: the labour of free manual, involuntary, non-rational marks. This is not a flight from figuration into abstraction (witness Bacon's own remarks on the 'sloppiness' of 'chancy abstract expressionism'[53]), but the development of a figure that is not irredeemably mired in cliché. Or, as Deleuze puts it, we have a 'first, prepictorial figuration', the clichés in the painter's head and on the canvas, the painter's initial intentions concerning what is to be done (for example, Bacon's intention in *Painting* to image 'a bird alighting on a field'). Then we have the emergence of the 'second figuration', the product of free, manual, involuntary or non-rational marks (for example, the umbrella that somehow emerges as part of the image in *Painting* by way of the lines that Bacon's hands follow, hands liberated from a preconceived narrative or intention, liberated from his mind's eye). So the figure we encounter emerges (perhaps a man, perhaps in a suit, perhaps sitting, a figure positioned beneath various cuts of butchered meat, the upper half of a head shadowed under an umbrella, the bottom half revealing a toothy grimace or grin). Again, and as Bacon himself says, it is not simply a matter of bird becoming an umbrella, of one representation or narrative replacing another, but the marks or lines suggesting a 'whole image'; the accident, and the autonomy of the accident or chance, becomes important as part of an immanently constitutive, self-forming activity or mode of thought. Of course, this 'second figuration' eventually becomes another figurative given, another tale (Deleuze refers to Bacon's *Painting* as a 'surrealistic tale' of 'head-umbrella-meat'[54]), but Deleuze's point here is that the emergence of a figure or an image such as we encounter in Bacon's *Painting* is, in the first instance, the 'reconstitution of a representation, the reconfiguration of a figuration', a pictorial or image-making act that is creative, a creative movement in thought or what he calls a 'leap in place'. Deleuze writes:

> there is a second figuration: the one that the painter obtains, this time as a result of the figure, as an effect of the pictorial act. For the pure presence of the figure is indeed the reconstitution of a representation, the reconfiguration of a figuration ... *A probable visual whole (first figuration) has been disorganized by free manual traits which, by being re-injected into the whole, will produce the improbable visual figure (second figuration).* The act of painting is the unity of these free manual traits and their effect upon and re-injection into the visual whole. By passing through these traits, figuration recovers and recreates, but does not resemble, the figuration from which it came.[55]

It is important from a Deleuzian perspective to think of the free manual marks as connected to what Bacon would call a 'graph' and what Deleuze calls the 'diagram'. As James Williams suggests, the diagram, for Deleuze, 'is the pre-figural preparation of the canvas, that is, the series of shades, colours, scratches and layers of material set down prior to the delineation of figure'.[56] So Bacon's free manual marks are always-already a diagram, or, perhaps more accurately, they are part of a diagramming activity that seeks to remove the figurative givens or clichés already present on the canvas. Diagramming is what Deleuze wants to call the 'act of painting' as such. 'It is precisely ... givens that will be removed by the act of painting, either by being wiped, brushed, or rubbed ...

For example, a mouth: it will be elongated, stretched from one side to the other. For example, the head: part of it will be cleared away with a brush, broom, sponge or rag'.[57] As is known, Bacon was a prolific painter of portraits and heads, and this is what Deleuze is obviously referring to here.[58] Deleuze's approach to Bacon's portraits and heads is, of course, philosophical; that is to say, he is interested in the concept of the 'head' that emerges from the Baconian act of painting. And yet, there is always, perhaps inevitably, a story to be told about this work. So, for example, Bacon's portraits and heads can quickly become a story, a narrative that essays or re-presents his relationships and involvements with: his lovers (Peter Lacy and George Dyer); fellow contemporary painters (Lucian Freud and Frank Auerbach); drinking partners (Muriel Belcher, Isabel Rawsthorne and Henrietta Moraes); friends (Bruce Bernard, John Hewitt); even intellectuals (Michel Leiris).[59] Deleuze is not concerned in the slightest with any such narrative, or with providing any kind of biographical backcloth to Baconian portraiture. Bacon, for Deleuze, paints and thinks a particular kind of concept of the head. Or, as he explicitly puts it:

> As a portraitist, Bacon is a painter of heads, not faces, and there is a great difference between the two. For the face is a structured spatial organization that conceals the head, whereas the head is dependent upon the body, even if it is the point of the body, its culmination. It is not that the head lacks spirit; but it is spirit in bodily form, a corporeal and vital breath, an animal spirit. It is the animal spirit of man: a pig-spirit, a buffalo-spirit, a dog-spirit, a bat-spirit ... Bacon thus pursues a very peculiar project as a portrait painter: to *dismantle the face*, to rediscover the head or make it emerge from beneath the face.[60]

This is an important passage, particularly for us as it connects the conception of the head found in Baconian portraiture explicitly to the idea of dismantling the face. Already we have come across Deleuze and Guattari's claim that the key function of painting is to actualize or think a deterritorialization of the face, and here we find the notion given more concrete resonance: *Bacon's portraits or heads effect a particular kind of deterritorialization of the face*. And this, it should be made clear, engenders a specific kind of Baconian ethics and politics. Remember for Deleuze and Guattari that if the 'aim of painting has always been the deterritorialization of faces' and if the face 'is a politics' (that is, a reductive and pernicious 'politics of recognition') precisely by being connected to a 'regime of signs' that can produce, sift and shape subjectivities on a sliding scale of conformity to a majoritarian norm, then painting immediately assumes another kind of ethico-political form, or, better still, painting is a visual form that can think and effect minoritarian becomings that are always-already ethico-politically disruptive by way of the movements they chart and the differences they make.

What is crucial here, then, is the deterritorialization of the face that is expressed through becoming-other, and in particular through Bacon's 'becoming-animal'. What am I talking about? Clear hints of the 'becoming-animal' of Baconian portraiture are already explicitly provided by Deleuze in the quote above. Thus when Deleuze stresses that Bacon's portraits and heads capture the corporeal or 'animal sprit of man: a pig-spirit, a buffalo-spirit, a dog-spirit, a bat-spirit ...' he is clearly gesturing towards a singularly Baconian notion of 'becoming-animal'. Once again, Deleuze stresses the crucial significance of the free manual marks, in particular, of the rubbing and brushing that 'disorganize the face', that 'make a head emerge', a head that marks 'traits of animality', where rubbing and brushing become 'spirits that haunt the wiped off parts, that pull at the head, ... the head without a face'.[61]

If any of this is beginning to sound like a rather vague spiritualism, then Deleuze immediately dispels such concerns by materially engaging specific works or paintings in order to set the concept of becoming-animal in motion. Some examples are worth briefly dwelling on here. For instance, in Bacon's *Triptych* of 1976 we have a head that gives way to the animal. But, and this is crucial from a Deleuzian point of view, it is not that the head simply resembles an animal as a form, it is that the work evokes certain 'animal traits', that the brushwork and scrubbing in a particular part of the canvas evokes and thinks the animal as a trait; the head becomes an animal trait – 'for example, the quivering trait of a bird'.[62] Or, in the *Triptych* of 1973, the animal is evoked or is thought by a spirit or shadow that autonomously escapes the body of the figure, like 'an animal we had been sheltering' Deleuze says.[63] Or, as in the 1968 work *Two Studies of George Dyer with a Dog*, an animal can be figured as such and become the shadow of its master, not in order for the painter to tell a story or draw any kind of formal correspondence between man and animal (for example, Dyer is an animal, Dyer is an animal lover, Dyer is my lover-animal), but rather to constitute, what Deleuze calls, 'a zone of indiscernibility or undecidability between man and animal'.[64] Man becomes animal, animal becomes man in Baconian portraiture not through the combination of forms and the production of differences that come to resemble something as yet unseen or unrealized (yes he is a man, but he is also a dog, a man-dog hybrid, oh now I see), but through the evocation of a certain commonality or deep identity between the two. What, then, is this commonality, this deep identity? For Deleuze, it is the *body* or, more particularly, the body 'insofar as it is flesh or meat'. Importantly, for Deleuze, the deep identity between man and animal as body or meat connects to an ethics and a politics, or the becoming-animal of Baconian portraiture always-already thinks *an ethics and a politics of the body as meat*. This is an ethics and politics grounded in an experience of suffering, perhaps we could even say in a shared sensation of suffering: the body suffers, that is, it experiences what we could call with Deleuze the 'intolerable'. And in its encounter with the 'intolerable' the body moves, or it is moved, to enter into becomings.[65] Deleuze makes these connections explicit when he writes that 'becoming-animal':

> is not an arrangement of man and beast, nor a resemblance; it is a deep identity, a zone of indiscernibility more profound than any sentimental identification: the man who suffers is a beast, the beast that suffers is a man. This is the reality of becoming. What revolutionary person – in art, politics, religion or elsewhere – has not felt that extreme moment when he or she was nothing but a beast, and became responsible ...[66]

If there is an ethics and politics in Bacon's becoming-animal it is an ethics and politics of encountering the intolerable, an encounter with bodily suffering, or a certain form of responsibility to engage and struggle with what is intolerable, even to evoke pity for the bodies that are found in an intolerable situation. This, clearly for Deleuze, is Bacon's lesson: 'Pity the meat! Meat is undoubtedly the chief object of Bacon's pity, his only object of pity, his Anglo-Irish pity'.[67] This is a tantalizingly odd, even provocative, notion that Deleuze confronts us with here. What does he mean by claiming that Bacon's painting express a kind of 'Anglo-Irish pity'? It is a tantalizing phrase because it immediately provokes us to speculate about the influence of the geo-political conditions in which Bacon finds himself, and it is odd because it seems to push us to interpret his work by way of a biography of these very geo-political conditions, to narrate or tell a biographical story, and this is a hermeneutical strategy that both Deleuze and Bacon want to discount, or at least problematize, from the very first instance. For if Bacon's work embodies a critical encounter with the cliché, and if the cliché circulates through the social by way of ready-made images and stories that speak through us in an anonymous fashion, then surely broad sweeping geo-political-biographical narratives fail to get us very far when encountering a singular body of work such as Bacon's? Let us focus on what Bacon himself says about the matter, again from his conversations with David Sylvester, when asked as to the reason why many people seem to detect in his work a 'distinct presence or threat of violence'. Bacon's reply, his use of language, is worth dwelling on here:

Well, there might be one reason for this, of course. I was born in Ireland, in 1909. My father, because he was a racehorse trainer, lived not very far from the Curragh, where there was a British cavalry regiment, and I always remember them, just before the 1914 war was starting, galloping up the drive of the house ... and carrying out manoeuvres. And then I was brought to London during the war and spent quite a lot of time there, because my father was in the War Office then, and I was made aware of what is called the possibility of danger even at a very young age. Then I went back to Ireland and was brought up during the Sinn Fein movement. And I lived for a time with my grandmother, who married the Commissioner of Police for Kildare ... and we lived in a sandbagged house and, as I went out, these ditches were dug across the road for a car ... or anything like that to fall into, and there would be snipers waiting on the edges. And then, when I was sixteen or seventeen, I went to Berlin ... I saw the Berlin of 1927 and 1928 ... which was, in a way, very very violent ... And after Berlin I went to Paris, and then I lived all those disturbing years between then and the war which started in 1939. So I could say, perhaps, I have been accustomed to always living through forms of violence – which may or may not have an effect upon me, but I think probably does. But this violence of my life, the violence which I've lived amongst, I think it's different to the violence in painting. When talking about the violence of paint, it's nothing to do with the violence of war. It's to do with an attempt to remake the violence of reality itself ...'[68]

This is a fascinating passage from a Deleuzian perspective. At first sight, Bacon clearly seems to want to set about telling his interlocutor a story about the geo-political conditions that are at play in his formative years (his Anglo-Irish movements, and the social-political turbulence of 1920s and 1930s Germany and France). And this is a story about the presence and threat of violence or, as he says, 'perhaps, I have been accustomed to always living through forms of violence'. And yet, it is interesting that Bacon's tone is really rather odd and tentative here ('So I could say, perhaps ...'). This tone is also present earlier in the passage when he says 'I was made aware of what is called the possibility of danger even at a very young age'. It is an oddly tentative and neutral expression, an expression that gestures toward anonymity I would suggest. And it is indeed tempting to think of such phrases as falling back on cliché, of words suddenly speaking through Bacon as he draws on a series of ready-made images and stories (for example, the early twentieth century turmoil of Anglo-Irish and Franco-German relations). Clearly, Bacon's discourse conforms to a narrative that could then be used by the biographer to contextualize the work. Simply put, Bacon's history and experience provide something of a biographical backdrop or explanatory framework within which to approach the paintings.

But, of course, Bacon then immediately dispels the notion. Yes, he acknowledges the violence of his own social-political conjuncture; yes, he even readily accepts that it may have had an effect upon him; but he categorically insists on a substantive difference between a particular social or historical experience of violence and 'violence in painting'. And his language is no longer tentative here; he wants to make himself absolutely clear. 'When talking about the violence of paint, it's nothing to do with the violence of war. It's to do with an attempt to remake the violence of reality itself ...'. So we see a key distinction emerge between geo-political conditions and a proximity to violence and the violence of painting as a medium in itself, the politics of which is expressed and thought through becoming as such; the remaking of the real, as Bacon would say. Painting, for Bacon, is not about showing or re-presenting the violent reality of the depicted scene. Painting has a constitutive relation to the real, or *it is real*, a violent reality of chance; the reality of an immanently constitutive self-forming activity that is thought in the image and through the medium of paint. If, as Deleuze says, 'Bacon's painting is ... a very special violence', then this violence has little to do with the depicted scene, or little to do with saying things about the depicted scene.[69] As Bacon puts it; 'I'm not saying anything. Whether one's saying anything for other people, I don't know. But I'm not really saying anything ...'.[70]


Bacon paints, he does not say anything! This is his lesson, a lesson Deleuze takes to heart, not only in relation to Bacon, but with regard to the very problematic of painting itself. In this chapter we have considered the Deleuze-Guattarian notion that the crucial function of painting is to deterritorialize or dismantle the face. This, as we have seen, is to always-already think an ethics and a politics, an ethics and a politics of minoritarian becomings, becomings that stand in extreme opposition to any politics of the gaze, or to any politics of recognition, which traffics in conformity to the majoritarian norm or submits to power assembled in the state-form. Hence the importance of Bacon's painting; hence the importance of Baconian portraiture as it expresses a specific kind of becoming: namely, becoming-animal. Key here is the deep identity between man and animal in Baconian portraiture, the deep identity between man and animal as body or meat. For if the ethico-political assumes a particular and concrete form in Bacon's work, it is precisely as *an ethics and politics of body as meat*, an experience of suffering, an experience of the intolerable that moves the body, or moves the body to enter into becomings ...

# 3 • Architecture

Just as Deleuze and Guattari confront us with the idea that language, literature and painting think the political, so too do they suggest that architecture thinks the political. That is to say, there is a politics of deterritorialization that is proper and peculiar to architecture or, more broadly put, built form, just as there is, for example, a politics of deterritorialization expressed through Kafka's literary experiments on the real, or Bacon's deterritorialization of the face. But what, though, is proper and peculiar to the politics of built form, or how does architecture as a form think the political? We shall see that one way to begin approaching this question is to think in terms of folds and forces, actually to think architecture as a kind of folding of forces, the political nature of which is expressed through the creation of a new political subjectivity, or what Deleuze and Guattari would call a 'new people'. In this way, architecture thinks the political to the extent that it is implicated in the formation of a new political subjectivity or a 'new people'. In their last collaborative work together, *What is Philosophy?*, Deleuze and Guattari refer to this notion of creating a people or forming a new political subjectivity as *fabulation* and they attribute to architecture, and to the arts more generally, a clear fabulating function. As we shall see, it is important to think of the fabulating function that Deleuze and Guattari generally attribute to the artwork – that is, the capacity of the artwork to invoke news forms of political subjectivity – as a kind of active political philosophy, as a form of thought that enters into a conjunction with the present milieu, but which nonetheless implies a deterritorializing politics; what Deleuze and Guattari explicitly call the 'utopian' gesture of calling 'for a new earth' as well as a 'new people'. We will encounter and develop this concept of fabulation in the second and, more particularly, third part of the chapter.

In the first part of the chapter, we will begin by more generally considering some of Deleuze and Guattari's comments on architecture and built form as they appear in *What is Philosophy?*. What will particularly emerge here is a concept of the 'house' which is immediately thought by Deleuze and Guattari to be an aesthetic form capable of creating 'sensations' – a concept of the house, or built form, that can subsequently be connected to what we can call an 'architecture of the outside' implied in 'virtual' time.

## House, Outside, Virtual

> Art begins ... with the house. That is why architecture is the first of the arts.[1]

It is interesting to note, with Ronald Bogue, that while Deleuze and Guattari write extensively on particular art forms (one automatically thinks, for example, of their long and sustained engagement with literature), their general reflections on the nature of the arts as such tend to privilege other forms that are perhaps treated less comprehensively in their work (consider painting, for example, and the importance of painting to their general reflections about the concept of an aesthetics of 'sensation').[2] This is also particularly the case with architecture as an art form. Although dealt with by Deleuze singularly in his books on Leibniz and Foucault,[3] and although Deleuze and Guattari often engage issues that are clearly of concern to students of architecture in their collaborative works such as *Anti-Oedipus* and *A Thousand Plateaus*,[4] it is nonetheless quite striking the extent to which architectural motifs begin to assume a particular significance to Deleuze and Guattari's general aesthetic reflections and to the cross-comparative analysis of different art forms that they undertake in *What is Philosophy?*. So if we were to engage Deleuze and Guattari at a certain level of generality – that is, if we are even to begin to attribute to them a broad and cross-comparative theory of the arts – then the architectural inevitably would assume significance as a vector or tendency in their aesthetic theory.[5]

So how does architecture figure in, or indeed frame, Deleuze and Guattari's general reflections on the arts, their aesthetic theory? At different points in chapter seven of *What is Philosophy?*, 'Percept, Affect and Concept', Deleuze and Guattari stress the idea that art begins in the carving out of a territory and in the construction of the house. For instance, in one passage Deleuze and Guattari speculate that the carving out of territory and the construction of a house begins with the animal or in the animal world, and what they call 'habitat' or the 'territory-house' system is always-already art, an art of gestures, colours, sounds; in short, a multiplicity of 'sensory qualities' that is immanently expressed in and through the construction of the 'territory-house'. Or, as Deleuze and Guattari explicitly state:

> Perhaps art begins with the animal, at least with the animal that carves out a territory and constructs a house (both are correlative, or even one and the same, in what is called a habitat). The territory-house system transforms a number of organic functions – sexuality, procreation, aggression, feeding. But this transformation does not explain the appearance of the territory and the house; rather it is the other way round: the territory implies the emergence of pure sensory qualities, of sensibilia that cease to be merely functional and become expressive … This emergence of pure sensory qualities is already art … It is an outpouring of features, colours, sounds that are inseparable insofar as they become expressive … Every morning … a bird of the Australian rain forests cuts leaves, makes them fall to the ground, and turns them over so that the paler, internal side contrasts with the earth. In this way, it constructs a stage for itself like a ready-made; and directly above, on a creeper or a branch, while fluffing out its feathers beneath its beak to reveal their yellow roots, it sings a complex song made up from its own notes and, at intervals, those of other birds that it imitates: it is a complete artist.[6]

So we see that for Deleuze and Guattari the house performs a territorializing function in carving out a territory, but that it never ends with the 'merely functional', that it becomes 'expressive' precisely because it implies the emergence of 'sensory qualities' (for example, the gesture of fluffing out the feathers, the colours of the paler leaves against the earth, the bird-song). It is important that we can extrapolate from this image of a 'territory-house' its immanently constitutive or self-forming power, what we could also call its *immediacy*. What does this mean? It may well help us to think again, for example, of Francis Bacon's work. For, as we saw in the previous chapter, the immediacy of an art form such as painting is expressed in and through the malleability of the medium itself;

that paint, as medium or form, is already malleability and 'chance', and no matter how wilfully or intentionally it is put on a canvas it still is, as a medium, an immanently constitutive or self-forming form. Again we can recall Bacon's comment: 'I mean you even don't know that when you put it on wilfully, as it were, with a brush – you never quite know how it will go on'.[7] Coming back to the Deleuze-Guattarian image of the 'territory-house' we could say that it too implies an aesthetic of malleable form, that the house is an immanently constitutive and self-forming form precisely because it is implicated in the construction of the 'sensibilia' (sounds, colours, postures) that gives it form. The sensibilia, or 'blocs of sensation' as Deleuze and Guattari call them, are always-already expressly thought in the built form, and the built form immediately sketches out what Deleuze and Guattari are content to call 'a total work of art'.[8]

By insisting that built form can 'sketch out a total work of art', Deleuze and Guattari obviously distance their idea of architecture from any kind of crude modernist functionalism, if by 'crude modernist functionalism' we mean that the function and form of what is constructed should follow from one another. As Deleuze and Guattari argue in the above quote, any functions which we may want to attribute to built form, or any functions that we may say a given built form can facilitate (for example, 'feeding', 'procreation') are themselves transformed in and through the construction of the built form, a transformation that locates the 'territory-house' in an implicative relation to function, and which cautions against the suggestion that built form can ever be seen as an 'appearance' or realized projection of any given functional requirement in advance of its construction as such. Put simply, we strictly never know what shape any given built form will take precisely because it is a malleable aesthetic form, composed of sensory qualities or 'blocs of sensation' (sound, colour) that co-emerge in and through the construction itself. Therefore, the function of any given building or built form (say, for example, the university office I am currently occupying while writing these words, or the lecture theatre in which I was teaching earlier today) quite literally functions in conjunction with certain sensory qualities that are expressed through it and which constitutively impact on its function (for example, the acoustics of the lecture theatre and, say, the extent to which they help or hinder the projection of my voice as the lecturer). Added to this, of course, is the problem that actually differing uses of any given building over time poses to the shape and form of its function as such (for instance, one of my favourite pubs in Belfast used to be a Presbyterian church).[9]

If there is a functionalism in Deleuze and Guattari's conception of built form, then it is a functionalism that must seek to approach the problem of a building's use through time, to acknowledge the potential for differentiation in use, function and consequently form. They hint towards this kind of functionalism at a couple of important junctures in *What is Philosophy?*. At one point, for instance, they insist on the notion of the house as a malleable aesthetic (again, the idea that it is a form that gives shape to sensory qualities or 'blocs of sensation') only 'on condition that it all opens onto and launches itself on a mad vector as on a witch's broom, a line of … deterritorialization …'.[10] What Deleuze and Guattari are gesturing towards here is a concept of built form that must stand in relation to an 'outside' – what we could call, in a slight modification of Elizabeth Grosz's terms, an 'architecture of the outside'. In what way, then, can we think through this notion of an 'architecture of the outside'? And how, more particularly, does a Deleuze-Guattarian 'architecture of the outside' connect to the problem of approaching the potential for differentiation in the use of built form through time? In order to begin unpacking these questions it will prove useful in the first instance to give consideration to Deleuze's *Foucault*, for it is here that we are clearly provoked to think the concept of the outside, and to think it in relation to certain architectural motifs. For instance, what Deleuze sees in Foucault's works such as *Raymond Roussel, Madness and Civilization, The Order of Things, The Birth of the Clinic* and *Discipline and Punish* is the development of a concept of the 'visible' that we could say implies an *architecture of light* as its real condition.[11] Foucault's work, Deleuze argues, provokes us with a concept of visibility that may at first sight seem paradoxical: that is, while visibilities are 'never hidden' they are 'nonetheless not immediately seen or visible'. Deleuze explains this in the following passage:

> For if … visibilities are never hidden, they are nonetheless not immediately seen or visible. They are invisible so long as we consider only objects, things, perceptible qualities and not the conditions which open them up …

> If different examples of architecture ... are visibilities, places of visibilities, this is because they are not just figures of stone, assemblages of things and combinations of qualities, but first and foremost forms of light that distribute light and dark, opaque and transparent, seen and non-seen ...
>
> *Discipline and Punish* describes prison architecture, the Panopticon, as a luminous form that bathes the peripheral cells in light but leaves the central tower opaque, distributing prisoners who are seen without being able to see, and the observer who sees everything without being seen ...[12]

What Deleuze is saying here apropos Foucault's architecture of light clearly connects to Deleuze and Guattari's idea of built form as a malleable aesthetic that is implicated in the construction of sensory qualities. Put simply, Foucault provides us with a notion of architecture which implies luminous sensation, the distribution of 'light and dark, opaque and transparent, seen and non-seen'. And we see that in mobilizing the term 'visibilities' Deleuze is provoking us to think beyond our everyday sense that the visible is anchored in objects and things, and to think in turn about the conditions in which our perception of objects/things is opened up, where this opening up involves an encounter with the idea that the visible is light itself; that there is a 'there is' of light, as Deleuze says, 'a being of light or a light being' that 'makes visibilities visible or perceptible'.[13] This is why Deleuze can make the seemingly paradoxical claim that while visibilities are 'never hidden' they are 'nonetheless not immediately seen or visible'. For example, in Foucault's Panopticon of *Discipline and Punish*, visibilities are 'never hidden' precisely because the architecture of the prison is distributing visibilities, perceptions, the seen and non-seen (that is, the peripheral cells are cast in light while the central tower remains opaque; and this leads to the consequent distribution of subjectivities where the prisoners are bathed in the light of the warden's gaze while the warden is cloaked in a darkness that implies the possibility of constant surveillance). In one way, then, the architectural visibilities of Foucault's Panopticon, the luminous sensations implied in and through it, are not hidden and are clearly related to perceptible or *felt* sensations (for instance, can I see the warden? Or, am I being watched?), which follow from its 'light-being' and which distribute subjectivities in accordance with a particular form of politics, the politics and power relations networked in the prison system as such. And yet, this politics, these power relations, are 'nonetheless not immediately seen or visible' as objects/things: rather, it is through the encounter with perceptible or imperceptible objects/things (luminous cells, opaque tower) that a particular architecture of light functions, an expressly political architecture which thinks, conditions and distributes bodies in a calculated, we could even say highly *stylized*, fashion.[14]

So how, then, do these ruminations concerning visibilities and the architecture of light in Foucault connect explicitly to the concept of the outside? 'Visibilities', Deleuze categorically asserts, 'must … be connected to the outside which they actualize',[15] and from this we can imply that an architecture of light or, in more broadly Deleuze-Guattarian terms, an architecture of sensibilia or sensation, connects to an outside that it actualizes. But what is the nature of this outside? Consider the following passage from *Foucault*:

> Foucault continually submits interiority to a radical critique. But is there *an inside that lies deeper than any internal world*, just as the outside is farther away than any external world? The outside is not a fixed limit but a moving matter animated by … folds and foldings that together make up an inside: they are not something other than the outside, but precisely the inside of the outside.[16]

The first thing that should strike us about Deleuze's comments here is that the spatial imagery seems paradoxical, intentionally paradoxical. For what can Deleuze mean by posing the question of whether there is 'an inside that lies deeper than any internal world', or an 'outside' that 'is farther away than any external world'? This seems immediately to render the notion of the outside rather odd, at least from the perspective of the spatial. How, to put the question pointedly, are we to begin to approach the concept of the outside if we rob ourselves of the spatial coordinates that help us limit and order our thoughts accordingly? This is Deleuze's provocation, and the provocation can be summed up with the following claim: *the outside is not simply a space as such.* This does not mean that the outside does not exist, that we can never quite grasp it, that it is impossible to experience it. Deleuze's point would indeed be the opposite: the outside does exist, and we can indeed experience it in felt sensations that can occur in and through time. Deleuze – by stressing the need for architectural visibilities to connect to an outside, or, as he says, 'actualize' the outside – wants immediately to temporalize the concept. Put all too simply, the concept of outside is always-already a temporal one, or is implicated in a particular conception of time; what the Deleuze of *Bergsonism* would call 'virtual' time.[17]

As all sensitive readers of Deleuze will recognize, the concept of the virtual as it is developed in *Bergsonism* and subsequently in works such as *Difference and Repetition* and *Logic of Sense* is a fundamentally important one; the 'principal name', as Alain Badiou puts it, of Deleuze's ontology and, consequently, it is a concept worthy of extensive treatment.[18] However, we will have to content ourselves by drawing out two rather general and related intuitions that follow from its treatment in *Bergsonism*, the purpose of which, of course, will be to fold these back into our concern here to clarify Deleuze and Guattari's 'architecture of the outside'. The first intuition is that time is positive and is experienced as a creation, as the making of a difference, as a construction of something new. Time is connected to an experience of the novel, a certain vitality or movement and change in the order of things. 'There is,' Deleuze wants to insist, 'a ... positivity of time that is identical to ... creation in the world'.[19] In a sense, the virtual nature of time, the virtuality of time if you will, is expressed in and through the experience of change, of making a difference, of the emergence of the new that is created and which disrupts an actually given order of things. This means, and this is the second general intuition, there is an important difference or distinction to be drawn out if we are to approach how the 'virtual' relates to any given 'actual' state of things or actual state of affairs. As Deleuze explicitly puts it:

> [I]n order to be actualized, the virtual ... must *create* its own lines of actualization in positive acts. The reason for this is simple: ... the actual does not resemble the virtuality it embodies. It is difference that is primary in the process of actualization – the difference between the virtual from which we begin and the actuals at which we arrive ... In short, the characteristic of virtuality is to exist in such a way that it is actualized by being differentiated and is forced to differentiate itself, to create its lines of differentiation in order to be actualized.[20]

As we see, Deleuze clearly wants to stress the positive difference that emerges in the passage from the 'virtual from which we begin and the actuals at which we arrive', that the virtual as such only exists 'in such a way that it is actualized by being differentiated', by being 'forced to differentiate itself'. Again, this implies the key idea that the virtual is expressed through a certain movement and vitality, through the positive difference that is created, the difference that makes a difference to the shape and form of any actual given order of things. In this sense, the virtual-actual couple implies an ontological difference or, better still, an ontology of differentiation and change that Deleuze would insist is freed from any predetermined logic of change. As is well known, one of Deleuze's key gestures in *Bergsonism* is to insist that we do not know what shape or form any given actualization of the virtual will take precisely because it is not a realizable possibility that can be projected in advance of its coming into being. Indeed, and in this Deleuze again follows Bergson explicitly, the very idea that one can unproblematically realize a possibility, or project the future realization of certain possibilities, is deeply flawed. For Deleuze, the concept of the possible is a 'false notion' or what he calls the 'source of false problems'.[21] Therefore, the projected future realization of any given possibility (for example, the projections in an architectural plan that would seek to envisage how the form of a given building will discharge predetermined functions) is an abstraction that cannot account for real change, the emergence of the new that is actually actualized in a given time. The idea of a projected future realization is an abstraction from the real because the real itself is implicated in virtual time, a time of unforeseen and unforeseeable differentiation, a time of change, change freed from a predetermined logic of change where 'everything is already given' in what Deleuze calls the 'pseudo actuality of the possible'.[22]

Let us now come back in a summary fashion to the idea of a Deleuze-Guattarian 'architecture of the outside'. From a Deleuze-Guattarian perspective, built form is and indeed needs to be connected to an outside which it actualizes. But what is this outside? It is not simply a space as such, but is implicated in time, a 'virtual' time of unforeseen and unforeseeable differentiation; a time of positive and productive change. Therefore, and in coming back to the related questions posed earlier, a Deleuze-Guattarian architecture of the outside, implicated as it is in virtual time, would see the problem of accounting for the potential for change and positive differentiation in the use of built form through time as something very important, and indeed unavoidable. Or, it is fundamental to any Deleuze-Guattarian conception of built form that acknowledgement is given to the problem of use, to the change and positive differentiation that is expressed through the plurality of functions to which the built environment may be put over time. For example, in a provocative and interesting article, 'Sensing the Virtual, Building the Insensible', Brian Massumi draws on Deleuze and Guattari to insist on the importance of stressing what he calls the 'life' and 'experience' of built form as it exists 'outside' of 'architectural design'. Architectural design can never simply be a projected realization of certain given possibilities and predetermined functions, or, rather paradoxically, it can only maintain this kind of abstract quality precisely by not being rendered concrete – that is, by not being built as such. For as soon as a building assumes a 'life', as soon as a building is built, it is experienced in what Massumi calls 'looking and dwelling', where 'looking' implies that the built form becomes an object that takes its perceptible place in the social-cultural landscape, and where 'dwelling' implies the passage of bodies that live in, work in, or otherwise move through it. Massumi writes:

> The outside of architectural design is in a very real sense its own product – the building itself; the life of the building. The building is the processual end of the architectural process, but since it is an end that animates the process all along, it is an immanent end. Its finality is that of a threshold that belongs integrally to the process, but whose crossing is also where the process ceases, to be taken up by other processes endowing the design with an afterlife. The most obvious after-processes are two: looking and dwelling. The exterior of the building takes its place as an object in the cultural landscape, becoming an unavoidable monument in the visual experience of all or most of the inhabitants of its locale. And the building becomes an experienced form of interiority for the minority of those people who live in it, work in it, or otherwise pass through it.[23]

What is interesting about Massumi's remarks in this context is the idea that the 'end of the architectural process' is an 'immanent end', the crossing of a 'threshold that belongs integrally to the process'. In other words, the 'outside' of architectural design is always-already and immanently expressed in and through the building itself; that the built form constitutes its own outside from the inside; that the outside is, in Deleuze's formulation quoted earlier from *Foucault*, 'precisely the inside of the outside'. Yet again, of course, we need to be alive to the importance of the virtual here, rather than simply getting caught up in the paradoxes of thinking the outside in spatial terms. For although Massumi is clearly suggesting that a building constructs its own spatialized and spatializing inside and outside (for example, the exterior that looks out and takes its place in social-cultural landscape, or the experienced interiority for those who populate its inside), his argument also thoroughly implies a commitment to the outside as implicated in 'virtual' time. How? For instance, when Massumi speaks to the idea of a given built form becoming something experienced (that is, 'becoming an unavoidable monument in the visual experience of all or most of the inhabitants of its locale', or as an 'experienced form of interiority for the minority of those people who live in it, work in it, or otherwise pass through it'), this experience is something that occurs, and must continue to occur, in a virtual time of change and positive differentiation. 'By virtual definition,' Massumi insists, 'the built form does not resemble its condition of emergence.'[24] So, to repeat the key point: if a built form is, as Massumi suggests, a form *experienced* in use and through time, then the form as experienced is at once implicated in the virtual as such; it becomes an experience of an always potentially new or positive differentiation that cannot be circumscribed or predetermined in advance.

## Folds, Forces AND Abstractions

By moving from Deleuze and Guattari's concept of the house as a malleable aesthetic form capable of creating 'sensory qualities' or sensations (colour, light, sound) to an 'architecture of the outside' implicated in 'virtual' time, the discussion above has undoubtedly remained at a rather abstract level, at least from a social and political perspective. And yet, architecture and, in its more expanded form, the built environment is, for Deleuze and Guattari, profoundly and irreducibly political. In a way, we have already hinted at this

with the notion of an 'architecture of the outside', and Deleuze and
Guattari's image of the house that 'opens onto and launches itself
on a mad vector as on a witch's broom', a built form that can trace
'a line of ... deterritorialization'. Put simply, there is a politics of
deterritorialization that is proper and peculiar to built form. But
what, though, is proper and peculiar to the politics of built form,
or how does architecture think the political? As was suggested at
the beginning of the chapter, one way to begin approaching this
question is to think in terms of folds and forces, to actually think
architecture as a kind of folding of forces, the political nature of
which is expressed through the creation of a new political subjectivity, or what Deleuze and Guattari would call a 'new people'. As
Deleuze categorically puts it in one interview:

> Architecture has always been a political activity, and any new architec-
> ture depends on revolutionary forces, you can find an architecture
> saying 'We need a people', even though the architect isn't himself a
> revolutionary ... A people is always a new wave, a new fold in the
> social fabric; any creative work is a new way of folding adapted to new
> materials.[25]

So we see that architecture is a form that is immediately both
aesthetic and political. As a 'creative work' architecture always-
already thinks the political because it is implicated in the
formation of a 'new fold in the social fabric', a new 'people' who
are given expression through the folding of forces. As has already
been said, Deleuze and Guattari would refer to this more generally
as the *fabulating* function of art; namely, the capacity of art to
invoke new forms of political subjectivity. In this regard, then, the
art-work can be seen as a kind of active political philosophy, a
form of thought that enters into a conjunction with its present
milieu, but which nonetheless implies a deterritorializing politics;
what Deleuze and Guattari call the 'utopian' gesture of calling 'for
a new earth' as well as 'a new people'.[26] I will inevitably come back
to this important notion of *fabulation* in due course, but, for the
moment, I want to further flesh out the basic intuition that architecture can be thought as the folding of forces. And in order to do
this it will prove useful to refer briefly to the work of Greg Lynn,
an architect and theorist who has been a key figure in mobilizing
the notion of the 'fold', and in articulating what it might mean to

talk about 'folding in architecture'.[27] By explicitly and consistently using the concept of the fold, Lynn has given a certain shape and form to the idea of a Deleuze-Guattarian architectural practice.[28] So, how, then, does folding take shape in built form? How can architectural practice express or embody a Deleuze-Guattarian notion of folding? Well, for Lynn 'folding in architecture' can be thought of in an almost culinary sense, say in the way a cake mixture implies a certain folding of ingredients, and where the folding integrates heterogeneous elements within a new continuous mixture. Or, as he explicitly puts it:

> If there is a single effect produced in architecture by folding, it will be the ability to integrate unrelated elements within a new continuous mixture. Culinary theory has developed both a practical and precise definition for at least three types of mixtures. The first involves the manipulation of homogenous elements; beating, whisking and whipping change the volume but not the nature of the liquid through agitation. The second method of incorporation mixes two or more disparate elements; chopping, dicing, grinding, grating, slicing, shredding and mincing eviscerate elements into fragments. The first method agitates a single uniform ingredient, the second eviscerates disparate ingredients. Folding, creaming and blending mix smoothly multiple ingredients ... in such a way that their individual characteristics are maintained. For instance, an egg and chocolate are folded together so that each is a distinct layer within a continuous mixture.[29]

Therefore, according to Lynn, folding implies multiplicity (for example, a variety of particular or individual ingredients) worked through a pliable and continuous mixture or form. Put another way, the pliability of the mixture or form is subject to forces outside itself (say, the hand of the baker and the repeated overturning or folding of the mixture) which it internalizes while retaining its difference (for instance, the heterogeneous elements of chocolate and egg, the distinct layering or stratification of these multiple parts). From the point of view of architectural practice, or built form, Lynn wants to experiment with this idea of internalizing outside or external forces in ways that allow for the production of difference. In other words, the outside or external forces that impact on built form can nonetheless be utilized in order to bring about its internal differentiation and continuous variation. In one sense, Lynn is offering us the possibility of a type of practice very much in tune with the concept of a Deleuze-Guattarian 'architecture of the outside' that was outlined above. Remembering that the outside is thought, again to quote directly from *Foucault*, to be 'moving matter', to be 'folds' that 'make up an inside'; that is to say, 'foldings' are 'not something other than the outside', but are 'precisely the inside of the outside'. So the potential internal differentiation and continuous variation of any given built form implies a folding that makes up an inside precisely through mobilizing outside or external forces in a way that differentiates them out. This is another way through which we could approach the problem of the continually various and pragmatically different uses that a built form can be subject to over time. As I said earlier, a favourite pub of mine in Belfast used to be a church; its inside, in one sense, became hollowed out or differentiated (out go the pulpit and the pews and in go the bar and the bar stools) and the external forces that impacted on this pragmatic re-appropriation of this inside space (for example, the religious constituency that the church served at a certain point no longer populated its surrounding locale, the church itself realized it could get a significant amount of money for what was a prime piece of real estate in a popular and increasingly 'trendy' urban locale) are, to use Massumi's Deleuze-Guattarian phrasing, 'virtual forces' generating the differentiation of the built form (that is, the church-becoming-pub as an expression of shifting economic and cultural-religious forces).[30]

As a practising architect, Lynn is interested in how this internal differentiation and continuous variation of built form can be facilitated in and through architectural design as such. Consider, for example, an architectural project that he first developed in response to an ideas competition for the city of Chicago in the early 1990s: what he called, 'The Stranded Sears Tower'. He describes the project thus:

> The Stranded Sears Tower attempts to generate a multiplicitous urban monument that internalizes influences by external forces while maintaining an interior structure that is provisional rather than essential ... This project attempts to reformulate the image of the American monument by reconfiguring the existing dominant icon on the Chicago skyline ...: the Sears Tower. The iconic status of the existing Sears

Tower arises from its dissociation from its context. The building establishes itself as a discrete and unified object within a continuous and
homogenous urban fabric. My project, by contrast, affiliates the structure of the tower with the heterogeneous particularities of the site while
preserving aspects of its monumentality: laying the structure into its
context and entangling its monolithic mass with local contextual forces
allow a new monumentality to emerge ...[31]

For Lynn, the Sears Tower is a monument to multiplicity, or a form
of monumentality that tends towards multiplication as such. The
tower is not a tower, but a number of towers; nine to be precise.
'The Sears Tower internalizes its multiplication by dividing itself
into a nine square tower that its engineer, Fazlur Kahn, has termed
the "bundled tube".'[32] Lynn wants to suggest that this 'bundled
tube' can further undergo 'a two-fold deterritorialization' in which
the building internalizes elements from the surrounding environment, while at the same time extending its influence outward into
the city.[33] In one sense, then, 'folding architecture' clearly expresses
no desire for a pure and clearly defined built form that abstracts
itself from its site and surrounding environment; what we could,
perhaps rather journalistically, call the desire for a decontextual-
ized modernism.[34] Built form needs to be connected to the site, to
engender affiliations to the site, to internalize the site as a series of
contextual forces; but, and this is crucial for Lynn, to do so in a
way that the built form is then differentiated and subject to multiplication. The built form is not a reflection of the site, not
conditioned by the site, nor is it designed to emphasize, say, the
contradictions that may play through the relation between the
built form and its site. Rather, the contextual forces outside the
built form and the affiliations of these outside forces to the built
form imply, again in Lynn's Deleuze-Guattarian terminology, a
'two-fold deterritorialization': the outside forces that blow a wind
– a little 'fresh air' as Deleuze and Guattari are often fond of saying
– through the inside, and the inside that shifts, changes and
extends through virtue of its connections to these outside forces.
Again we can quote Lynn directly:

> The project reformulates the vertical bundle of tubes horizontally along
> a strand of land between Wacker Drive and the Chicago River adjacent
> to the existing Sears Towers. The nine contiguous tubes accommodate

themselves to the multiple and often discontinuous borders of the site
... These ... engender affiliations with particular local events – adjacent
buildings, landforms, sidewalks, bridges ... and river's edge – that
would have been repressed by a more rigid and reductive geometric
system ... The ... internal order of the bundled tube ... is differentiated
by the external forces of the river's edge, the city grid, and the vectors of
pedestrian and transportation movement. The bundled tube is a
possible paradigm for a multiplicitous monument. It is an assembly of
microsystems that constructs an icon that is provisional. Examined
closely, the unified image of the monument unravels into heterogeneous
local events ... The Stranded Sears Tower is neither discrete nor
dispersed, but rather turns from any single organizational idea toward a
system of local affiliations outside itself.[35]

Lynn's stress here on a 'folding architecture' animated by affiliations and connections to outside forces is also strongly echoed in
the work of another key Deleuzian or Deleuze-Guattarian theorist
of architecture and urbanism; namely, John Rajchman. Indeed, one
of the key intuitions in Rajchman's provocative and seductively
written book *Constructions* is that Deleuze is an architectural
thinker of connections, a thinker of the AND.[36] Those familiar with
Deleuze's work will recognize that Rajchman, in stressing the
importance of this notion of the AND, is seeking to mobilize
Deleuze's self proclaimed 'empiricism'. We can consider, for
example, Deleuze's preface to the English translation of *Dialogues*
for a clear indication of what he means by 'empiricism'. 'I have
always felt,' Deleuze announces in the very first line of the preface,
'that I am an empiricist, that is, a pluralist.'[37] But what, then,
connects empiricism to pluralism, or what makes the empiricist a
pluralist? Deleuze gives the following answer: 'It derives from two
characteristics by which Whitehead defined empiricism: the
abstract does not explain, but must itself be explained; and the aim
is not to discover the eternal or the universal, but to find conditions under which something new is produced (*creativeness*)'.[38] Put
simply, empiricism implies pluralism to the extent that it aims to
foreground the conditions of 'creativeness'. In this way, 'pluralism'
is another term that Deleuze uses in order to express his key ontological intuition about the positivity of difference in creation, the
difference that makes a difference to the actually given, the difference that is – again to adopt the formulation from *Bergsonism*

used earlier – 'identical to creation in the world'. It is important to see how this second characteristic of empiricism always-already implies the first. In other words, in order to explore or interrogate the conditions in which something new can be created or brought into being (we could call this the creative side of Deleuze's empiricism), it is imperative to explain or to be alive to how certain notions of the abstract, how certain forms of abstraction, enter into and subsequently shape thought (we could call this the critical side of Deleuze's empiricism).

Both the critical (that is, the interrogation of abstractions or forms of abstract thought) and creative (that is, the difference or pluralism expressed through the creation or production of the new) sides of Deleuze's empiricism imply a logic of the AND, a logic of connections and becoming, as opposed to a logic of the IS, or a logic of 'being'. The key here, from a Deleuzian perspective, is to approach 'things' not in terms of predicates (for example, This IS a building!), but in terms of the multiple connections that make up the thing, and the multiple connections that are yet to be made outside our present sense of what the 'thing' is (for instance, the virtual forces that are connectively at play in the changing functions and form of a building, or the as yet unforeseen connections a given built form can enter into in the future). In his very first book on Hume, *Empiricism and Subjectivity*, Deleuze sums up this logic of connections or the AND with the following formula: 'Relations are external to their terms'.[39] In other words, when things enter into connections, when things form conjunctions and relations, they do so on the outside; and on the outside the terms change or, better still, the terms assume a new form in light of the conjunction or connection they have entered into. Deleuze urges us as follows:

> Substitute the AND for the IS ... The AND is ... not a specific relation or conjunction, it is that which subtends all relations, the path of all relations, which makes relations shoot outside their terms ... and outside everything which could be determined as Being, One, or Whole ... Relations might still establish themselves between their terms ..., but the AND gives relations another direction, and puts...terms...on a line of flight which it actively creates. Thinking *with* AND, instead of thinking IS ...: empiricism has never had another secret. Try it, it is a quite extraordinary thought ...[40]

As already implied, it is precisely this Deleuzian idea of thinking with the AND that Rajchman wants to try out in the context of his discussion of architecture and urbanism in *Constructions*. For example, he describes the idea of a 'virtual house' as the 'one which through its plan, space, construction, and intelligence, generates the most connections', a built form that is 'so arranged or disposed as to permit the greatest power of unforeseen relations'.[41] Or he suggests a notion of 'future cities' as so many 'virtual futures' that 'precede our given identities' and 'our possible relations with one another', further stressing that the 'virtual futures' of the city are 'always invisible' precisely because 'their actualizations always involve a departure from known or foreseeable identities'.[42] So we see that through these gestures Rajchman is clearly following the logic of the AND, gesturing toward a concept of becoming and the virtual that is thought to be implicated or folded into the IS, but which can also be explicated or differentiated out of the IS. Let us come back again to the example of my local pub. It IS a pub, those of us who use it know what it is and we know what it will remain for the foreseeable future – the pub has Being in this sense. And yet, the pub as it IS can be thought to be the product of a series of relations or virtual forces that have been connected up, actualized and differentiated out in a particular way (for example, the relation or conjunction of the cultural-religious, economic and demographic forces that are at play in its transformation from church to pub). This relation or conjunction of forces precedes our given identification of the pub as it IS now, while also bearing witness to a logic of the AND; a virtuality or vitality that can be expressed in the yet to be determined or, as Rajchman says, 'invisible' future of the new conjunction.

If Rajchman is keen engage the creative side of the Deleuze's empiricism (where the logic of the AND implies the conjunctive or connective conditions in which the new or difference is produced), he is equally alive to what we have called its critical side. Rajchman follows Whitehead's injunction to critically interrogate the abstract, to explain how abstractions give shape and form to thought and also, perhaps crucially, to explore whether a positive and productive concept of abstraction is worth arguing for. Taken together, then, Rajchman's is an empiricism that implies both a critique and a rethinking of abstraction, a critique of how we have come to think abstraction and a reconstruction or the painting of 'another picture

of what it is to think abstractly'.[43] Clearly, there is a certain provocation in Rajchman's insistence on the need to 'think abstractly'.
For why should we deal in abstractions? Should we not try to understand the world in which we find ourselves in the most 'concrete'
terms possible? This kind of response or question is particularly
banal and stupid, and for an important reason. The crude valoriza-
tion of the 'concrete' and the denunciation of the 'abstract' never get
us very far in thought, unless and until we begin to recognize that
abstractions are always-already concretized in thought, giving
shape to it.[44] Rajchman is particularly interested in picturing the
relation that abstract thought may have with arts such as architecture and how, more generally, we can mobilize a Deleuzian
empiricism to rethink the function of abstraction in the arts.
Immediately, he wants to caution against the idea that abstraction is
negative; an abstraction of 'Nots', as he would call it. In other
words, he wants to challenge the notion that abstraction in the arts
should be seen in terms of a process of negative emptying out, a pure
form without content, a virgin canvas, a blank page. On this view,
the abstract 'is what is *not* figurative, not narrative … to the point
where one arrives at a sanctifying negative theology in which "art"
… takes the place of "God" as That to which no predicate is ever
adequate and can only be attained *via negativa*'.[45]

Against a negative theology of the 'not', Rajchman asserts his
Deleuzian empiricism by insisting on an 'abstraction of the
"and"'.[46] Again we need to immediately think this notion in terms
of a critical and creative empiricism; that is, a critique of the
abstractions that shackle thought or render it immobile, but also
its creative or affirmative rethinking. Rajchman captures this
double movement of Deleuze's empiricism in the following
passage, which is worth quoting at length:

> One might then say that there are two sorts of abstractions in Deleuze,
> two senses of what it is to abstract and to be abstract. The first is the
> Platonic sense of abstract Form. It is the object of the 'critique of
> abstractions' … that Deleuze … formulates when … he declares, 'The
> abstract does not explain, but must itself be explained'. To explain *by*
> abstractions is to start with abstract Forms and ask how they are real-
> ized in the world … But to explain those abstractions themselves is to
> reinsert them in a … 'pluralistic' world that includes multiplicities that
> subsist in Forms and induce variations in them, altering their connec-

tions with other things. In this way one shows that they are abstract in the invidious sense of being incapable of complication or movement – such is the critique. Thus one attains a complicated condition in things prior to Forms ... and ... one arrives at another question: not how are Forms ... realized in things, but under what conditions can something new or singular be produced 'outside' them? Thus one comes to the second sense of the abstract in Deleuze – the sense of the 'and' that moves outside. To pass from the first critical sense of the abstract to this second 'affirmative' one is to transform the very idea ...[47]

Let us try to review the momentum of Rajchman's argument here. First, Deleuze's empiricism implies a critique of abstractions that would shackle and immobilize thought, abstractions that are 'invidious' precisely because they are 'incapable of movement' – and here Rajchman implicates the abstraction of the 'Platonic Form'. This gesture echoes the explicit critique that Deleuze and Guattari make of the Platonic Form or Idea in their concluding remarks on what they call the 'abstract machines' of *A Thousand Plateaus*. 'There is no abstract machine', they say, 'in the sense of a Platonic Idea, transcendent, universal, eternal'.[48] For Rajchman, the Platonic Form is 'invidious' or 'incapable of movement' to the extent that it posits itself and concerns itself with the question of 'how it is realized in the world'. Here Rajchman's remarks tend toward Deleuze's *Bergsonism*, or Deleuze's Bergsonian critique of the 'real-possible' couple, where the 'real', or the process of realization, is always-already determined in advance by the concept it is said to bring into being, where 'everything is already given', again to quote Deleuze, in 'pseudo actuality of the possible'. In other words, the posited concept (for instance, Plato's concept of the Form) remains an 'invidious' abstraction for as long as it determines in advance the world it is said to be realized in (say, for instance, the political world of Plato's *Republic* where the Form of Justice determines in advance a class system governed by the intellectual classes, Plato's famous 'philosopher-rulers').[49] Against this invidious abstraction of the Form we have an empiricism critically sensitive to the 'multiplicities that subsist in Forms and induce variations in them, altering their connections with other things'. And this, of course, is abstraction of the 'and', the multiplicity of forces that play through and 'outside' Forms as they become mobilized and shifted in new and unforeseen conjunctions.

## From Deleuze and Guattari's Abstractions to the Concrete of Belfast

I want to begin this final part of the chapter by staying with (and hopefully developing in my own way) Rajchman's very helpful distinction between the two kinds of abstraction that he rightly sees at play in Deleuze and Guattari's thinking. As I implied in the preceding section, in *A Thousand Plateaus* Deleuze and Guattari play with the conceptual couple 'abstract-concrete' in their concluding chapter 'Concrete Rules and Abstract Machines', reinforcing the idea that abstraction can be something positively affirmed in the production or creation of difference. Indeed, the very idea of an 'abstract machine' immediately conjures images of production and construction, an abstraction that can and must be made, rather than an abstraction we posit uncritically, or an abstraction that does our thinking for us. In this way, Deleuze-Guattarian abstractions or 'abstract machines' do not necessarily stand in opposition to some notion of the 'concrete'; rather, 'abstract machines', as they say, 'operate in concrete assemblages'.[50] Put simply, the labour of abstraction is, for Deleuze and Guattari, always-already a concrete labour, the work of the AND, of making the connections and assembling differences that make a difference to what is actually given. So we have a potential labour of abstraction (the assemblage of a difference that makes a difference), but we also have the dangers involved in resting content with the abstractions that do our thinking for us (thoughts or concepts that have been immobilized or reified, or only function to immobilize or reify thought as IS). It is important to point out, again with Rajchman, that these two forms of abstraction imply a complicated and complicating politics, or any given social-political formation or environment will, in actuality, combine both these forms of abstraction.[51]

Consider with me, in this regard, my home town of Belfast. Clearly, much ink has been spilled in essaying the complications of Belfast as a social-political formation. Here I will keep my remarks relatively brief and particularly focused on aspects of the political geography and built environment that I think connect to the forms of abstraction to which Rajchman's Deleuzian empiricism is critically sensitive.[52] In terms of 'invidious abstractions', the kind of abstractions that prevent, stultify, reify, immobilize or simply frustrate critical thinking, one could begin by speaking in rather general terms of a desire to abstract or literally get out of a troubled history of political conflict. In Belfast and beyond there has been much recent talk (mainly journalistic or media speak) of the notion of a 'post-conflict' Northern Ireland – that is, an expressed wish and belief that we are seeing the emergence of a public sphere or an experience of public life that is no longer primarily shaped by the antagonisms generated by acts of politically motivated violence.[53] Of course, it is important to point out that this very understandable desire for abstraction from a troubled history of political violence is not peculiar to the supposedly 'post-conflict' politico-institutional conjuncture of the 'present'.[54] Rather, it is something that inevitably coexists historically with 'the troubles' itself, an abstraction that has always operated through what we could journalistically call the 'height of the troubles' – that is, the experience of violence that marked the 1970s, 1980s and 1990s. Let me give you what I hope will be a concrete sense of what this might mean from my own experience: a very brief insight into one small aspect of the political geography and built environment of the Belfast that I grew up in.

Born in 1972, I grew up in an area of Belfast called 'the village'. This was and still is a predominantly working-class 'protestant' and 'loyalist' area. Connected by a small through-road or avenue called 'Broadway', the village at this time flowed seamlessly into what is now the predominantly working class 'catholic' and 'republican' area of the Falls Road in the west of the city. As ethno-political tension and sectarian violence increased in the city in the 1970s, Broadway became a flashpoint area, a space of possible and often actual antagonism and conflict (say, for example, youths caught up in the banal repetition of stone throwing, rioting, fighting). This changed quite dramatically in the late 1970s and early 1980s with the building of a dual carriageway that, in effect, bisected the village and Falls Road, obliterating almost at a stroke Broadway as a space that had previously facilitated this particular kind of ethno-political antagonism. This dual carriageway, 'the westlink' as it was called, was completed in February 1981.[55]

Clearly, we can think of the development of the westlink as a rather literal concretization or even ideological reproduction of the developing sectarianism in the Belfast of the time (that is to say, as a form of segregationist ideology built in concrete). But it is not just that. Using again the Deleuze-Guattarian language of Rajchman's urbanism, I would say that there is a logic of abstraction immanent to the concrete assemblage of the westlink as such. How so? At once we can see it as a concretized desire for abstraction from conflict and political antagonism. In this sense, the westlink concretizes the idea of a public space that promises a depoliticization of space, or at least a neutralization of sectarian space, literally cutting the flow (the flow expressed in and through Broadway) of ethno-sectarian violence. Of course, this does not mean we should simply level an explicit accusation at the door of Belfast's urban planners of the late 1970s, or simply see them as conscious agents of a State ideologically immersed in the problem of managing the developing conflict. To repeat, the westlink need not simply or exclusively be viewed as the ideological reproduction of a sectarian politics or, in this case, as the ideological concretization of the State's response to managing sectarian antagonism. Coming back to Deleuze-Guattarian principles, it is important to emphasise that built form can never simply be a site of crude ideological reproduction; for it is also a malleable aesthetic capable of creating sensations that are peculiar to the form itself.

Thinking back to the multiplicity of sensations that impacted upon me as a child and young adult negotiating this urban space, one thing in particular becomes strikingly clear; namely, that traversing or moving through the westlink at Broadway on foot was a particularly precarious and risky act. There are two points worth emphasizing here. First, and most obviously, in bisecting Broadway, cutting off its flow between the village and Falls Road areas, the dual carriageway creates a sensation of an 'over there'. So, from my perspective as someone living in the 'loyalist' village, the Falls Road end of Broadway becomes a clearly discernible 'over there', concretized as a foreign and potentially dangerous 'republican' space. Second, and more interestingly from a Deleuze-Guattarian perspective, the actual built form of the dual carriageway expresses this precariousness, this sensation of engaging in a perilous and risky act. There was the obvious sensation of negotiating the mass of traffic the carriageway carried. A safer walk from the village end of Broadway to the Falls Road end involved the negotiation of a huge roundabout that carried all the traffic south of the city into the city centre, and all traffic north of the city to the south. This, as I implied, was safe and negotiable on foot, but only via a number or network of crossings that made the walk a much more involved process than it had previously been. In order to avoid this roundabout way of getting across I remember walking rather swiftly or indeed running across the carriageway when a lull in the traffic permitted it. And this rather precarious and risky act was made ever more difficult because the ground at this crossing point was layered in concrete that spiked out of the ground; concrete that was clearly built to discourage anyone from negotiating it on foot. I remember more than once nearly turning my ankle at this crossing ...[56]

To be sure, the westlink is a concrete assemblage, but is no less an abstraction for that, an abstraction that concretizes the idea of a depoliticized or neutralized public space. In this way, and since its inception, the building of this dual carriageway connects to the contemporary notion of Belfast as a 'post-conflict' city; a city whose public spaces are supposedly no longer dominated by the antagonisms generated by politically motivated violence. The implication here, of course, is that the westlink can be seen concretely to embody an abstraction that is 'invidious' in Rajchman's sense, an abstraction that immobilizes thought in a certain way, an abstraction that thinks for us, an abstraction that flows through the social-political formation without ever really being interrogated as such. What do I mean? Well, clearly, the very notion of Belfast as a 'post-conflict' city is itself an 'invidious' abstraction, the constant ideological reproduction of which is mediated to its own citizens predominantly through a local print and broadcast journalism intent on continually emphasizing a 'new' Belfast of political progress and 'peace'.[57] Dressed in the garb of a well-meaning but thoroughly uncritical journalism, this image of Belfast as a 'post-conflict' city does not simply mask or cloak the reality of a city still deeply divided and segregated on ethno-political lines.[58] It also, perhaps more importantly, permits a new kind of politics as such, what we could call a *politics of social and economic development*. For there is a strong connection between the twin narratives of political progress and social-economic development in contemporary Belfast, or contemporary Belfast has itself become a story in which political progress and social-economic development are folded into one another.[59]

It is hardly surprising in these circumstances that the built environment or urban geography of Belfast has become a site –

perhaps the site – of this new politics of social-economic development. Indeed, at the time of writing, the westlink of my youth and
young adult life is currently undergoing dramatic reconstruction
and further development.[60] Two things are immediately worth
emphasizing about this current change. First and most obviously,
perhaps, the development is very much locked into the narrative of
the political progress of Belfast as a 'post-conflict' city. Second and
fascinatingly, from a Deleuze-Guattarian perspective, there is the
explicit political sanctioning of the idea that the 'post-conflict' city
can itself be aesthetically mediated and foregrounded in and
through its newly built environment. In this regard, it is important
to note that in 2005 Belfast City Council commissioned a public
artwork or sculpture to be built on the newly developed westlink
at Broadway. Initially, the competition was won by a Californian
artist Ed Carpenter who proposed creating a forty-five metre high
public sculpture called 'Trillian'.[61] Described in the local press as a
'wild bloom' or 'flower' to symbolize the 'regeneration' of a 'post-
troubles city', Carpenter's own description of the project neatly
folds into this narrative of political progress. Consider his
following statements to the local media in Northern Ireland at the
time:

> It represents germination for the future ...

> It represents growth, transformation, evolution, and these are all
> subjects which are universal and which we can identify with and partic-
> ularly in a city which has had some negative press around the world ...

> It will provide a ... very optimistic and memorable large scale monu-
> ment which will be visible from a great distance night and day and
> which can be identified with by the people of Belfast ...[62]

Of course, while it is all very well to be critical about the contemporary political configuration of Belfast as a regenerated
'post-troubles city', the danger is always that we end in cynicism, a
cynical critique that never really goes anywhere: this is the cynicism of the 'fireside revolutionary' as Marx would say.[63] To be
sure, it makes sense to essay the connections between a piece of
built environment such as the westlink and broader, and indeed
'invidious', abstractions such as the 'post-troubles city', but it is
equally important that we retain something of the Deleuze-

Guattarian idea that built form or the built environment can be an aesthetic medium capable of a politics of deterritorialization. Earlier in the chapter it was suggested that architecture or built form is at once aesthetic and political precisely because it is, as Deleuze would say, a 'creative work' implicated in the formation of a 'new fold in the social fabric', or a 'new people' who are given expression through the folding of forces. This, as was stated, brings to mind what Deleuze and Guattari would more generally call the *fabulating* function of art, which is the capacity of art to invoke new forms of political subjectivity; the notion that art can operate as a kind of active political philosophy, a form of thought that enters into a conjunction with its present milieu, but which nonetheless implies its deterritorialization. I now want to revisit and hopefully render this notion more concrete against the backdrop of my discussion about the westlink in Belfast; to speculate, therefore, as to whether a piece of built environment such as this can be thought of in relation to a different kind of abstraction – an 'affirmative' rather than 'invidious' abstraction, to again use Rajchman's terminology.

In its own way, Carpenter's 'Trillian' always-already implies a tendency to think a particular kind of deterritorialization as soon as it embodies the idea of a city 'flowering' anew, one capable of 'growth' and 'transformation', a very concrete and thoroughly 'optimistic' symbol of a brighter, better, more prosperous future. As I implied above, it is perhaps all too easy to be cynical about this, or curmudgeonly in how one responds to it. Yes, we could dismiss such politically sanctioned public art as naive or utopian. Yes, 'Trillian' is an abstraction connected to an image of a 'post-troubles city' that seems naïve and utopian when set against the backdrop of the very real segregationist and sectarian geography of the city. But, perhaps we miss an important point here; perhaps we miss the point of the importance of the self-consciously abstractive gesture of building such a piece of public sculpture. Perhaps we actually need to push the logic of this a little further; perhaps the problem here is not naivety or utopianism, but the right kind of utopianism. In *What is Philosophy?*, Deleuze and Guattari distinguish between two types of utopia and emphasize the importance of what they call 'immanent, revolutionary, libertarian utopias'.[64] Drawing on Adorno and Samuel Butler, Deleuze and Guattari stress that this kind of utopia is not an abstraction from the real, but more of an abstraction that is immanent to the real. Rather than being a 'no-where', Deleuze and Guattari insist that 'utopia' signifies an immediate connection with the forces of the milieu or environment in which it is expressed; 'utopia' as a gesture toward what they call the 'now-here'.[65]

Let us return, then, to Belfast, to the Broadway roundabout, to speculating about the possibility that a piece of public sculpture or public art can connect to the social-political forces pulsing through the milieu or environment in which it is given expression. What would this piece of public art look like? When considering the social and political forces that pulse through the Broadway round-about one is, of course, immediately moved to think in terms of the social and economic development of Belfast as a 'post-troubles city'. This seems obvious enough, but what is perhaps less obvious are the ways in which these and other forces are themselves differ-entiated out, or how they have been folded in various ways through time. Here we must come back to Massumi's idea of how a built form is experienced in 'dwelling' and how the experience of a built form is an experience mediated in and through its prag-matic use as such. Of course, most people traverse the Broadway roundabout in their cars moving, at times, at great speeds and with little or no real sense for the space beyond an instrumental one of reaching a destination. This, clearly, is different for the people who have lived in close proximity to the space through its past and present development. We are in a different temporal register here, a certain slowing down in the experience of the space as it were. As someone who grew up there, it will always be a space of memory for me (for example, the vague recollections of the construction work in the late 1970s, or the vague recollections of playing in the 'bog meadows' or land on which the dual carriageway was subse-quently built, or my clearer recollections of negotiating the space as a teenager in the late 1980s when I needed to go, say, to buy new football boots at the shops located 'over there' towards the Falls Road end of Broadway), even if I pass through it in the car at speed.

Different experiences of the space; different ways of dwelling in the space; different modes of temporality encountered in and through the space; different forms of consumption of and in the space. Broadway as a roundabout one passes through to get to where one wants to go, a space consumed at speed and with a feel only for the facilitation of such passage. Broadway as a site of memory; as a space to be negotiated on foot for the purposes of shopping, a space experienced as a site of sectarian antagonism that lasted years, a space whose flow along Broadway has been cut off at a certain point in time and will always be experienced as 'cut off'.[66] So while it is clear that the development of the Broadway roundabout and the westlink more generally has, since its inception and ever more so in the present conjuncture, been shaped by the forces of social and economic development (and by the promise of being part of a 'post-troubles city' abstracted from sectarian antagonism), these forces and the developments shaped by them are negotiated differently, folded into different bodies of people, producing different modes of subjectivity. And the pragmatic use of the space is therefore marked by the kind of continual variation that Deleuze and Guattari talk about in relation to the pragmatics of language. That is to say, we could almost speak of the architectural grammar of the space as never given, but as always subject to variation via its performative use as such. So, the question now becomes: can a piece of public art, sculpture or some kind of monument located at this site respond to the differentiation or multiplication of the space as performatively used?

In *What is Philosophy?*, Deleuze and Guattari emphasize the importance of what could be called a *dematerialized* or *abstract monument*. They think of the monument as something that stands up, that preserves something, what they call a 'compound of sensations'. What matters here for Deleuze and Guattari is not the preservation of the material form or medium through which sensations are expressed, but the sensations themselves, for the sensations are the monument as opposed to the built form in which they are given expression: 'Standing up alone does not mean having a top and a bottom or being upright (for even houses are drunk and askew); it is only the act by which the compound of created sensations is preserved in itself – a monument ...'.[67] I think we can take this idea of created sensations in a monument that is dematerialized and abstract and begin speculatively to run with it in the context of Broadway.[68] Say, for instance, we envisage a monument not to sight and looking graspable across the city, but a monument to sound that implies occupancy or dwelling in the space. Say we envisage the construction of a radio mast capable of broadcasting certain sounds within a five or six mile radius of the site. What kind of sounds? Well, what about short two- to three-minute narratives of the experiences of the different bodies or constituencies of people who have and continue to use the space in question; past and present commuters, residents, shoppers, workers and so on? What I am suggesting here, of course, is that the monument (radio mast) functions through a kind of demateri-alization as sound (the narratives of those who have used the space); that these sounds as narratives essay and think aloud the ways in which those using the space have negotiated the social, economic, political and historical forces that have given shape to their experiences and how these forces have been bent, folded and refolded through this very use. So, I could envisage myself as a participant in this project, thinking about or recalling my own experiences of negotiating the space and the shifting modes of subjectivity implied or differentiated out of this negotiation; sensa-tions of risk, precariousness, of being 'cut off' from 'over there'.[69]

If the envisaging of this very particular and geographically specific kind of project at Broadway seems a far cry from the kind of *fabu-lating* and deterritorializing function Deleuze and Guattari generally attribute to the artwork, then I think this is only the case if we assume that the creation of a 'new earth', a 'new people' or new forms of political subjectivity needs to be some dramatic or other-worldly gesture. But it need not be, for Deleuze and Guattari's idea of a 'new earth' or 'new people' needs, as they insist, to be thought in terms of a 'utopianism' of the 'now-here' and there is nothing elusive or mystical about the assumption of a new form of political subjectivity. It can be as small (and as big) as a shift in subjective attitude and thinking, a different take on the social and political world that one inhabits, and a corresponding shifting in the meanings we then attribute to the very concepts of the 'social', 'political' and 'world'. And this, of course, is the very thing that Deleuze and Guattari insist that architecture, built form, or art more generally, is capable of through *fabulation*. If this *fabu-lating* function of art implies abstraction, it is an 'affirmative' abstraction in Rajchman's sense; an abstraction of the 'and', a concrete labour, a desire to assemble a difference that makes a difference to what is given in the present milieu. What kind of difference would our envisaged project at Broadway make to the subjective attitudes and thoughts of those who participated in the production and consumption of work? What kind of connections would it allow those who encounter the work to think and make in interpreting and evaluating the forces pulsing through the space they occupy? These are crucial or critical questions from a Deleuze-Guattarian perspective.[70]

# Conclusion

As I said in my introductory remarks, this short book was intended to perform a two-fold function: (a) to give a feel for some of Deleuze and Guattari's writings on the arts and (b) to extrapolate from these writings the idea that thinking the political, that political theory if you like, can have aesthetic form. Or, put another way, that the arts as such can be thought to be forms of political theory. The general intuition here, to repeat, is that the arts always-already are forms of political theory to the degree that they actively exercise their capacity or autonomy to think the political and, in so doing, shift the meanings we may subsequently attach to the 'political'. We have seen this intuition implicitly and explicitly at play all throughout the book, in and through Deleuze and Guattari's writings on language, literature, painting and architecture. Let us review some of the momentum of this argument.

In chapter one, we confronted the Deleuze-Guattarian idea that language and literature are always-already political. Drawing on Deleuze and Guattari's philosophy of language in *A Thousand Plateaus*, we saw how they insisted on the power, vitality – in short, the autonomy – of language to intervene directly in and give shape to our social-political world. Central to this image of language is the idea of the 'order-word' or 'slogan', and these terms through Deleuze and Guattari's usage come to signify the capacity of language not simply to re-present or communicate information about our social-political world, but to shape it in an expressly material way. It is important to appreciate and acknowledge that Deleuze and Guattari's own writings, their style of expression if you will, embody the intuition that the order-word or slogan functions coextensively in and through language-use. Put simply, Deleuze and Guattari's writings are a form of sloganizing and, by literally writing against representation, they performatively and autonomously enact the very critical method they employ. Think back, for example, to Deleuze and Guattari's statements in *A Thousand Plateaus* concerning the efficacy of 'ideology' as a critical concept. As we saw in the first part of chapter one, Deleuze and Guattari's statements on ideology are exemplary in performatively enacting and bringing to life the idea that language functions through the issuing of order-words or slogans. Rich in perlocutionary effect, they force the reader to re-evaluate and shift their thinking on ideology: for example, away from any crude economic determinism to a theory of ideology that interrogates the ways in which, as Deleuze and Guattari say, 'expressions and statements intervene directly in productivity, in the form of a production of meaning or sign-value'.[1]

So, if language has a capacity and power to intervene directly in the political, if it can shape the meaning we attach to the 'political' as such, then this obviously implies that our very concept of the political, the political concepts we use in investing meaning or significance in our world, assume a form that is constituted in language-use. As we saw in the second and third parts of chapter one, this intuition very much informs the way in which Deleuze and Guattari engage bodies of 'literature' such as Kafka's. In *Kafka* Deleuze and Guattari are expressly concerned to emphasize the political thinking that is expressed in and through his writing. Two points are worth re-emphasizing to underscore this suggestion. First, we saw that Kafka's concept of the political is immediately connected to a form of writing that is 'comic' or 'humorous' where, for example, political authority is subject to a comic or humorous exaggeration and critique; a 'becoming-molecular' as Deleuze and Guattari say. Second, we saw that political concepts such as 'Law' become subject to a critique in a Kafka novel like *The Trial* to the extent that they are caught up in a movement that is defamiliarizing or, in Deleuze-Guattarian terms, 'deterritorializing'. Again it is important to emphasize that Deleuze and Guattari consider Kafka's writings as something that embodies – that performatively and autonomously enacts – this movement: a 'deterritorialization of the world that is itself political'. Put simply, Kafka's writing or use of language does not simply mediate the political by commenting, for example, on how the law works or ought to work; it directly and immediately thinks the political through the movements it charts, the concepts it creates and, consequently, the deterritorializations it brings about.

In moving from Deleuze and Guattari's writings on language and literature to their writings on painting we witnessed this continued emphasis on the deterritorializing potential of the arts. Of course, the deterritorializations effected in and through painting are different or particular to the medium in question. Indeed, and as I attempted to demonstrate in chapter two, Deleuze and Guattari are specifically interested in the way that painting functions to deterritorialize or 'dismantle' the 'face', and in the way this dismantling or deterritorialization of the face implies or thinks a particular concept of ethics and politics. It is in this context that the importance of Francis Bacon's work can be re-emphasized. From a Deleuze-Guattarian perspective, Bacon's paintings effect a deterritorialization of the face and, in so doing, imply or think an ethics and politics of 'minoritarian becomings', becomings that counter any politics of the gaze, or any 'politics of recognition', which traffics in conformity to 'majoritarian' norms or submits to 'Power' in the 'state-form'.

Key here, as we have seen, is Baconian portraiture and the singularly evocative notion of 'becoming-animal' that emerges from Bacon's portraits and heads. Or, more particularly, it is crucial to be sensitive to how Bacon's painterly ability to bring to life a 'becoming-animal' implies or thinks an ethics and a politics of the *body as meat* and an experience of the 'intolerable' that moves the body to enter into becomings. Once again, the stress here should be on how a medium such as painting is poorly understood for as long as we rest content with the idea that it trades in images that simply re-present, communicate or mediate the reality of minoritarian becoming. Bacon's painting, Deleuze insists, is always-already caught up in a form of minoritarian becoming; it is immediately caught up in this very deterritorializing movement to the extent that it sets things in motion through the 'violence' of certain painterly techniques – for example, the 'free manual marks' actualized in and through brushing, rubbing, scratching, throwing paint.

The arts do not simply mediate the real through commentary or representation; *they are real* to the degree that they participate in, or precipitate, a certain movement in the order of things. As we have seen, this idea of movement and change can be connected to what Deleuze and Guattari would call 'fabulation', a kind of active political philosophy that functions to call forth what they call a 'new earth' or a 'new people'; that is, to create or think new forms of political subjectivity. Of course, one of the gestures I made in the third and final chapter was to essay the connection between this very notion of 'fabulation' and architecture or, more broadly, built form. If architecture is an art or form capable of fabulation, then this is because it can create 'blocs of sensation' or can 'fold forces' in order to bring about a shift in our sensibilities regarding the social and political world we inhabit.

Importantly, Deleuze and Guattari insist that the fabulating and deterritorializing function they generally attribute to the art-work, and to particular forms such as architecture, should be approached in terms of a 'utopianism' of the 'now-here' and that there is nothing elusive, dramatically heroic or other-worldly about the assumption of a new form of political subjectivity. As was suggested at the end of chapter three, the assumption of a new form of political subjectivity can be as small (and as big) as a shift in subjective attitude and thinking, a different take on the social and political world that one inhabits, and a corresponding shifting in the meanings we then attribute to the very concepts of the 'social', 'political' and 'world'. And this, of course, is precisely what is politically significant about the art-work; its capacity to bring into being or think concepts of the 'social' and 'political' that force us to shift our very thinking, that force us to think these notions of 'social' and 'political' differently. Art-works as so many slogans that cut right to the heart of what we have seen Deleuze and Guattari call the 'production of meaning or sign-value'.

So what, if any, are the implications that follow from extrapolating from Deleuze and Guattari's writings on the arts the idea that political theory can have aesthetic form? Why, to pose the question slightly differently, is it important to argue for the idea that the arts can and should be seen as forms of political theory?

To emphasize the capacity, indeed autonomy, of aesthetic forms such as literature, painting and architecture in thinking the political and in shifting our sense of what the very term 'political' may mean is, I think, a useful lesson and reminder to us – by 'us' I particularly mean those of 'us' who are paid a salary to do 'political theory' – that political concepts can come in many different forms, and that a critical sensitivity to these differences is a crucial acknowledgement of the pluralism of political thought itself.[2] At one point in *A Thousand Plateaus* Deleuze and Guattari say that they 'have been criticized for overquoting literary authors' and they immediately respond to this accusation by arguing that 'when one writes, the only question is which other machine the literary machine can be plugged into'.[3] This is Deleuze and Guattari at their pluralistic best as they immediately reject the idea that somehow the aesthetic form (in this case literature) simply mediates the real, or lacks a reality that other forms of thought (say, philosophy, science or 'political science') may have. The aesthetic form is always-already real; real in its political function, real in being plugged into a changing, shifting political reality that co-emerges through its expression as such (we could again think, for example, with Deleuze and Guattari about the 'Law' or the 'bureaucratic machine' with which Kafka confronts us and how Kafka's writing and thinking forces us to think these ideas differently).[4]

In one sense, we could say that Deleuze and Guattari are offering us the resources to think through an *aestheticization of political theory*, where this is obviously taken to imply a critical sensitivity to the productive role the arts can play in shaping and shifting the meanings we assign to the 'political', and where this positively implies a critical openness to the pluralism of political thought itself.

I think it is important before concluding to acknowledge that this suggestion of a Deleuze-Guattarian aestheticization of political theory is itself obviously open to possible critique. For instance, it could be argued that aestheticizing political thought is deeply problematic because it implies a rather vague crypto-normativism that importantly risks remaining abstracted from the real rough and tumble of actual social-political life. Or, perhaps to put the critique more directly and forcefully, a deterritorializing politics such as we find in Deleuze and Guattari's writings on the arts implies that we should *value* movement and change, the emergence of a 'new people' or shifts in subjectivity (hence the crypto-normativism), but that these notions of movement, change, or a 'new people' remain curiously vague and are therefore abstracted from the concrete normative prescriptions that are required by social and political actors who are concerned actually to change the world. 'By posing the question of politics ... in the apocalyptic terms of a new people and a new earth,' argues Peter Hallward for instance, 'Deleuze's philosophy amounts to little more than utopian distraction' and consequently remains 'essentially indifferent to the politics of this world.'[5]

While Hallward clearly wants to critique Deleuze's concept of
the political because he believes that it implies 'utopian' ideas, intuitions and values that are less than clear or normatively
prescriptive at the level of strategic action,[6] he nonetheless misses
an important point about how Deleuze and Guattari think the
utopian, their 'utopianism' of the 'now-here'. The 'utopianism' of
the 'now-here', as already stated, is not necessarily elusive, dramatically heroic or other-worldly, but must, under Deleuze and
Guattari's insistence, be connected to the forces of our world, the
forces that are negotiated in the shaping and shifting of political
subjectivity. Rather than reading Deleuze and Guattari's writings
on the arts (or their writings more generally) for normative
prescriptions to guide political action, it is important to be sensitive to their pragmatics of the slogan, indeed to see their call for a
'utopianism' of the 'now-here' as a slogan, a rallying cry that forces
us to confront the forces at play in our immediate environment.[7]
Hallward, I think, underestimates the power and vitality of
Deleuze and Guattari's pragmatics and the extent to which the
aesthetics of the written form (or aesthetic forms more generally)
are embodied and can be folded into bodies in social-political life.[8]
I, on the other hand, have tried to make a play of this here, for
example, in the third and final chapter where I engaged Deleuze
and Guattari's writings on architecture, connected them to their
concept of a 'utopianism' of the 'now-here' and folded it into some
of my own experiences and reflections on the forces that have
come to shape the political geography and built environment of
my home town; Belfast. I did this not in order to legitimize or
valorize my own 'concrete' experiences, but precisely to explore
the idea of a Deleuze-Guattarian 'abstraction' of the AND; that is, a
labour of making connections or a desire to assemble a difference
that makes a difference to what is given in the present milieu.
Thus, in my case, this simply meant *using* Deleuze and Guattari to
think critically about how the political geography and built environment of Belfast functions to concretize the notion that it is
somehow a 'post-conflict' city.[9]

# Notes

## Introduction

1  Clearly, then, this book does not pretend to be an exhaustive account of Deleuze and Guattari's writings on the arts. For such a comprehensive overview, see Roland Bogue's impressive three volume work, *Deleuze on Literature*, (New York, 2003), *Deleuze on Music, Painting and the Arts* (New York, 2003), *Deleuze on Cinema* (New York, 2003). I will often have occasion to draw implicitly and explicitly on Bogue's invaluable work here throughout.

2  The reader will note the modest scope of the work undertaken here; that, for example, I will make no mention of Deleuze's sustained engagement with cinema. Of course, this is not to imply that cinema as a form is somehow incapable of thinking the political or bringing to life political concepts. Indeed, and as I have argued elsewhere, cinema needs to be acknowledged as a form which thinks the political, and thinks it autonomously on its own cinematic terms. See Robert Porter, *Ideology: Contemporary Social, Political and Cultural Theory* (Cardiff, 2006); Robert Porter, 'Habermas in Pleasantville: Cinema as Political Critique', *Contemporary Political Theory*, 6, 4 (2007), pp. 405–18.

3  Gilles Deleuze and Félix Guattari, *A Thousand Plateaus: Capitalism and Schizophrenia* (London, 1988); Gilles Deleuze and Félix Guattari, *Kafka: Toward a Minor Literature* (Minneapolis, 1986).

4  Deleuze and Guattari, *Kafka: Toward a Minor Literature*, p. 10. For a fuller explanation of this important point, see the second part of chapter one.

5  For a fuller explanation of this important point, see the third and final part of chapter one.

6  This point is most particularly developed in the second part of chapter two.

7  This point will be developed towards the end of the final part of chapter two.

8  For a fuller discussion of the connection between minoritarian becoming – 'becoming-animal' in particular – and Bacon's use of 'free manual marks', I refer you to the third and final part of chapter two.

9  This gesture is made and developed in the second and third parts of chapter three.

¹⁰  On the idea that architecture creates 'blocs of sensation', see particularly the first part of chapter three.

¹¹  On the idea that architecture implies a 'folding of forces', see particularly the second part of chapter three.

¹²  For a good appreciation and articulation of this intuition, see, for example, Michael J. Shapiro, *Deforming American Political Thought* (Lexington, 2006); Jon Simons, 'Ideology, Imagology, and Critical Thought: The Impoverishment of Politics', *Journal of Political Ideologies*, 5, 1, (2000), pp. 81–103.


## Language and Literature

¹  Gilles Deleuze and Félix Guattari, *A Thousand Plateaus: Capitalism and Schizophrenia* (London, 1988); Gilles Deleuze and Félix Guattari, *Kafka: Toward a Minor Literature* (Minneapolis, 1986).

²  Deleuze and Guattari, *A Thousand Plateaus*, pp. 75–76.

³  The coinage 'order-word' is Brian Massumi's translation of *mot d'ordre*, which literally means 'words of order', but is perhaps rendered most concrete by the term 'slogan'. Indeed, Jean-Jacques Lecercle suggests that 'order-word' is a rather 'bizarre coinage' that is unhelpfully abstract and potentially depoliticizing as it tends to suggest that orders simply issue from the individual or subject who enunciates, whereas *mot d'ordre* understood as a 'slogan' is always political and always presupposes a collectivity, or what Deleuze and Guattari would call a 'collective assemblage of enunciation'. See Jean-Jacques Lecercle, *Deleuze and Language* (Basingstoke, 2002), p. 169. I have decided to keep Massumi's coinage for the moment, but I will explicitly connect 'order-word' or *mot d'ordre* to the notion of the 'slogan' later on in the chapter.

⁴  Deleuze and Guattari, *A Thousand Plateaus*, p. 76.

⁵  Deleuze and Guattari, *A Thousand Plateaus*, p. 76.

⁶  Deleuze and Guattari, *A Thousand Plateaus*, p. 76.

⁷  What I am trying to hint at here is a broadly Bergsonian conception of the cliché, where language freezes or orders the world, subjects it to interest and common sense. For a good discussion of this Bergsonian idea, and for a clear recognition of how Bergson's thinking on language has influenced Deleuze, see Lecercle, *Deleuze and Language*, pp. 25–26.

⁸  Hobbes's classical statement of the need for a strong state and law and order is, of course, to be found in his most famous work *Leviathan*. See Thomas Hobbes, *Leviathan* (London, 1968).

9   Deleuze and Guattari, *A Thousand Plateaus*, p. 77.
10  Deleuze and Guattari, *A Thousand Plateaus*, p. 78.
11  Deleuze and Guattari, *A Thousand Plateaus*, p. 78.
12  The difference here between the pragmatics of Deleuze and Guattari
    and the 'universal pragmatics' of Habermas is striking. Deleuze and
    Guattari would not accept the Habermasian intuition that language-
    use – the famous 'communicative action oriented to mutual
    understanding' – is structurally determined and conditioned by an
    always-already implied intersubjective reciprocity. For a possible
    Deleuze-Guattarian critique of Habermas on this point, see R. Porter
    and K. A. Porter, 'Habermas and the pragmatics of communication: A
    Deleuze-Guattarian critique', *Social Semiotics*, 13, 2 (2003), 129–45.
    For a positive elaboration of how Habermasian pragmatics may be
    mobilized in expressly more political terms as a critique of ideology,
    see Robert Porter, *Ideology: Contemporary Social, Political and
    Cultural Theory* (Cardiff, 2006), pp. 36–51.
13  Deleuze and Guattari, *A Thousand Plateaus*, pp. 79–80.
14  Following Nietzsche, Deleuze asserts that meaning, the 'sense' and
    'value' we have of things, is always-already force, or the composition
    of the forces that take possession of that thing. See Gilles Deleuze,
    *Nietzsche and Philosophy* (London, 1986). For an excellent discussion
    of this idea, see Brian Massumi, *A User's Guide to Capitalism and
    Schizophrenia: Deviations from Deleuze and Guattari* (London,
    1993).
15  Deleuze and Guattari, *A Thousand Plateaus*, p. 81.
16  Deleuze and Guattari, *A Thousand Plateaus*, p. 81 and 89.
17  Deleuze and Guattari, *A Thousand Plateaus*, p. 4.
18  On this point, see Lecercle, *Deleuze and Language*, p. 171.
19  'It would be an error to believe that content determines expression by
    causal action, even if expression is accorded the power not only to
    "reflect" content but to react upon it in an active way. This kind of
    ideological conception of the statement, which subordinates it to a
    primary economic content, runs into all kinds of difficulties ...'
    Deleuze and Guattari, *A Thousand Plateaus*, p. 89.
20  From a Deleuzian and Deleuze-Guattarian perspective, there is a sense
    in which all questions can be viewed as rhetorical, as presupposing or
    indeed inventing answers that always-already function pragmatically
    as imperatives ('Surely Deleuze and Guattari are wrong ...!' Is this not
    a clear example of Deleuze and Guattari's staggering naivety when it
    comes to the theory of ideology!'). For example, in *Difference and
    Repetition*, Deleuze highlights the way a question can pragmatically
    'force the one response which always continues and maintains it'. See
    Deleuze, *Difference and Repetition* (London, 1994), p. 195. This, at

least in part, explains Deleuze's philosophical distaste for questions, for any kind of philosophy based on a communicative model of question and answer. 'Most of the time, when someone asks me a question, even one which relates to me, I see that, strictly speaking, I don't have anything to say. Questions are invented, like anything else. If you aren't allowed to invent your questions, with elements from all over the place, from never mind where, if people "pose" them to you, you haven't much to say'. Gilles Deleuze and Claire Parnet, *Dialogues* (London, 1987), p. 1. For a fuller discussion of the implications that follow from Deleuze and Guattari's pragmatic analysis and critique of the imperatives, or even violence, implied by the question, and a helpful appreciation of how Deleuze and Guattari have been influenced here by Canetti's *Crowds and Power*, see Jean-Jacques Lecercle, *The Violence of Language* (London, 1990), p. 46.

[21]   Of course, the power of Deleuze and Guattari's intervention or slogan 'There is no ideology and never has been' is hardly exhausted by the particular disruption it caused to the 'Althusserian' assumptions I initially carried to the text of *A Thousand Plateaus*. Such an anecdotal suggestion is meant to immediately hint at a broader 'collective assemblage of enunciation' at play in certain circles of political and cultural theory in UK universities at that specific conjuncture. Simply put, Deleuze and Guattari set this 'collective assemblage of enunciation' in motion, upsetting the patterned actions and thoughts of those working out of a Marxist tradition that somehow had become seduced by a representationalist base/superstructure model. Indeed, to associate this representationalist thinking with Althusser, or to refer to my own thinking as expressive of a kind of 'vague and unthinking Althusserianism', is itself far from unproblematic. The vagueness and lack of reflexivity is mine not Althusser's, well not even really 'mine', but part of the collective assemblage as expressed through cliché. Further, it is important to point out that Deleuze in particular is concerned to praise Althusser's work, not to bury it. For example, in *Difference and Repetition*, Deleuze makes an explicit point of affirming Althusser's reading of Marx's *Capital*. Althusser's 'structuralist' Marxism is praised precisely because it departs from a representationalist logic, whereby the 'economic' is assumed pre-given and actually determined in advance. Read through a Deleuzian lens, the Althusserian concept of 'the economic' is never properly given in actuality, but is always 'a differential virtuality to be interpreted'. Put simply, 'the economic' is determined differentially by the 'problems' it continually poses for social-political analysis and critique, rather than by any solution it determines in advance. See Deleuze, *Difference and*

*Repetition*, p. 186. Also, see Peter Hallward, *Out of This World: Deleuze and the Philosophy of Creation* (London, 2006), p.49.

22  As I have tried to show elsewhere, a number of influential contemporary ideology theorists – Michael Freeden and Paul Ricoeur are two good examples – would share the basic intuition that ideology will always be part of the reality of social-political life precisely because what we understand and negotiate as the 'real' is always-already ideological, or ideologically predetermined in some way. In affirming what I called a 'critical conception of ideology', and by drawing on Jürgen Habermas, Slavoj Žižek and Deleuze and Guattari in different ways to constitute such a notion, I challenged and set out to critique the idea that the reality of social-political life is always-already ideological. See Porter, *Ideology: Contemporary Social, Political and Cultural Theory*, pp. 131–7. Although, I should say that now as I look back at this work I feel decidedly uncomfortable with how I tried to make this argument function, as I tended to employ certain rhetorical devices which too conveniently fell back on supposedly transcendental and universal claims that are, in the end, flatly stated, rather than critically interrogated. Indeed, or from the perspective of a Deleuze-Guattarian pragmatics, my argument in favour of a 'critical conception of ideology' in the conclusion of the book sloganizes in the name of a universalism and transcendentalism that is assumed rather than critically accounted for.

23  Deleuze and Guattari, *A Thousand Plateaus*, p. 84.

24  Deleuze and Guattari, *A Thousand Plateaus*, p. 89.

25  See Porter, *Ideology: Contemporary Social, Political and Cultural Theory*, pp. 91 and 98–100.

26  Gilles Deleuze and Félix Guattari, *Anti-Oedipus: Capitalism and Schizophrenia* (London, 1984), p. 28.

27  Deleuze and Guattari, *Anti-Oedipus: Capitalism and Schizophrenia*, p. 28.

28  Deleuze and Guattari, *Anti-Oedipus: Capitalism and Schizophrenia*, p. 101.

29  So where linguists tend to analyse language in accordance with a law of identity, in terms of what Deleuze and Guattari would called 'constants', a pragmatic approach necessitates we track the 'lines of continuous variation' that language-users actualize in specific concrete instances (for example, the word 'ideology' as it appears on this page of *Anti-Oedipus*, or that passage in *A Thousand Plateaus*). Further still, Deleuze and Guattari think that the potential language has for 'continuous variation' as a kind of 'virtual' potential, fully real and yet never exhausted by any actual or given form of language-use as such. In this way, the claim or statement that, say, 'I think ideology as a

concept is best thought of as ...!' has a virtual existence on a continuum of potential actualizations, out of which will emerge a usage that tends towards constancy only to the degree it is enforced through regular patterns of action. So, the virtual potential for continual variation comes first, constants or identity being extracted or subsequently abstracted from this virtuality after. 'It is possible to take any linguistic variable and place it in variation following a necessarily virtual continuous line ...', Deleuze and Guattari, *A Thousand Plateaus*, p. 99. For a helpful discussion and deceptively clever contextualization of this point, see Roland Bogue, *Deleuze on Literature* (New York, 2003) pp. 98–100.

30  Deleuze and Guattari, *Kafka: Toward a Minor Literature*, pp. 41–2.

31  More particularly, there is no maintainable distinction to be made between Kafka's supposedly 'private' letters and his short stories and unfinished novels. For none of these components of Kafka's 'literary or writing machine', as Deleuze and Guattari call it, are defined by any kind of intentional public/private split in terms of publishing or public consumption. Kafka's 'private' letters are part of the 'literary machine', communicating as they do with the short stories and unfinished novels. 'Kafka's work is not defined by a publishing intention. Kafka evidently did not think of publishing his letters; quite the contrary, he thought of destroying everything he wrote as though it were like the letters. If the letters really are part of the work, it is because they are an indispensable gear, a motor part for the literary machine as Kafka conceives of it ...'. Deleuze and Guattari, *Kafka: Toward a Minor Literature*, p. 29. For a helpful discussion of how the components of Kafka's writing machine cut across and communicate with one another so as to disrupt any simple demarcation of 'art' and 'life' in Kafka, see Bogue, *Deleuze on Literature*, pp. 86–9.

32  It is important to acknowledge that the work of Deleuze and Guattari has provoked feminist thought in a number of interesting ways, ranging from oppositional critique to creative mobilization. For a most impressive survey of various feminist engagements with Deleuze and Guattari, and for one of the most striking and compelling examples of a positive and creative mobilization of Deleuze and Guattari in light of feminist concerns, see Dorothea Olkowski, *Gilles Deleuze and the Ruin of Representation* (Berkeley, 1999).

33  Richie Robertson, for example, rather emphatically suggests that Kafka was 'overwhelmed by his father'. Drawing on Kafka's diaries, Robertson points to the fact that 'Hermann Kafka's massive body', his 'noisy self-confidence and absolute authority made him seem like a giant' to the young Franz. He thinks it important to mention that Kafka's father could 'devour' food 'piping hot, in large mouthfuls,

crunching the bones', using this information as a prelude to speculating that these images of the father are at the 'origin of the many brutal flesh-eating characters in Kafka's fiction'. See Richie Robertson, *Kafka* (Oxford, 2004) pp. 6–7.

34  Kafka wrote his 'Letter to the Father' in November in 1919 and there is a tendency, even in relatively sophisticated Kafka scholarship, to take it at face value as a private piece of discourse – that is, a son analysing the type of relationship he has with his father – which nonetheless ends in the kind of self-analysis and personal revelation that can be used in uncovering the reasons why Kafka began writing the kind of 'fiction' he did. For an example of such reading, see Ronald Hyman, *A Biography of Kafka* (London, 1981), p. 245. Also see Robertson, *Kafka*, p. 5.

35  Deleuze and Guattari, *Kafka: Toward a Minor Literature*, p. 9.

36  Deleuze and Guattari, *Kafka: Toward a Minor Literature*, p. 9.

37  Kafka writes: 'Often I picture a map of the world spread out and you lying across it. And then it seems as if the only areas open to my life are those that are either not covered by you or are out of your reach …'. Quoted in Hyman, *A Biography of Kafka*, p. 245.

38  Deleuze and Guattari, *Kafka: Toward a Minor Literature*, p. 10.

39  Deleuze and Guattari, *Kafka: Toward a Minor Literature*, p. 10.

40  'This can occur because the comic amplification … discovers behind the familial triangle (father-mother-child) other infinitely more active triangles from which the family itself borrows its own power, its own drive to propagate submission …'. Deleuze and Guattari, *Kafka: Toward a Minor Literature*, p. 11.

41  Franz Kafka, *The Transformation and Other Stories* (London, 1992), pp. 76–126.

42  The first lines read: 'When Gregor Samsa awoke one morning from troubled dreams he found himself transformed in his bed into a monstrous insect. He was lying on his hard shell-like back and by lifting his head a little he could see his curved brown belly, divided by stiff arching ribs, on top of which the bed-quilt was precariously poised and seemed about to slide off completely. His numerous legs, which were pathetically thin compared to the rest of his bulk, danced helplessly before his eyes'. Kafka, *The Transformation and Other Stories*, p. 76.

43  Deleuze and Guattari, *Kafka: Toward a Minor Literature*, pp. 35–6.

44  Kafka, *The Transformation and Other Stories*, p. 76.

45  The notion of Deleuze and Guattari's work embodying a kind of 'fleshy materialism' is one I appropriate from Peter Hallward. Although, he uses the term to signify what he considers a rather misplaced tendency in the secondary literature on Deleuze. For rather

than understanding the work of Deleuze and of Deleuze and Guattari in terms of an embodied or 'fleshy materialism', Hallward impressively builds the case for a 'spiritualist' or 'theophanic' Deleuze, a Deleuze whose work 'is essentially indifferent to the politics of this world'. See Hallward, *Out of This World: Deleuze and the Philosophy of Creation*, p. 162. I will return to Hallward's critique in the concluding chapter.

46   Kafka, *The Transformation and Other Stories*, p. 101.

47   Kafka, *The Transformation and Other Stories*, p. 76.

48   Gilles Deleuze, *Spinoza: Practical Philosophy* (San Francisco, 1988); Gilles Deleuze, *Expressionism in Philosophy: Spinoza* (New York, 1992).

49   'The becoming-animal effectively shows a way out, traces a line of escape, but is incapable of following it or making it its own ...'. Deleuze and Guattari, *Kafka: Toward a Minor Literature*, pp. 36–7. This does not necessarily mean that all forms of 'becoming-animal' remain blocked or problematic from an ethico-political point of view. Indeed, and as we shall see in the next chapter, there is a 'becoming-animal' expressed through Francis Bacon's painting that implies what we will call an ethics and politics of the body as meat. See particularly the final part of chapter two.

50   'Everything that the world requires of impoverished people they fulfilled to the utmost; his father fetched breakfast for the minor officials at the bank, his mother sacrificed herself making underwear for strangers, his sister ran up and down behind the counter at the bidding of customers ...'. Kafka, *The Transformation and Other Stories*, p. 111.

51   Kafka, *The Transformation and Other Stories*, p. 115.

52   Simon Critchley, in a different context, writes engagingly about the ethico-political importance of the 'smile', of 'laughter' and 'humour', showing how it can, as he says, bring about a 'change of situation', a 'surrealization of the real' that challenges power, making us 'realize that what appeared to be fixed and oppressive is in fact the emperor's new clothes, and just the sort of thing that should be mocked and ridiculed'. See Simon Critchley, *On Humour* (London, 2002), pp. 10–11.

53   'Gregor's metamorphosis' is a 'story of a re-Oedipalization that leads him into death, that turns his becoming-animal into a becoming-dead'. Deleuze and Guattari, *Kafka: Toward a Minor Literature*, p. 36.

54   Deleuze and Guattari, *Kafka: Toward a Minor Literature*, pp. 46–7.

55   Deleuze and Guattari, *Kafka: Toward a Minor Literature*, p. 47.

56   Bogue, *Deleuze on Literature*, p. 80.

57   Bogue, *Deleuze on Literature*, p. 81.

58   Deleuze and Guattari, *Kafka: Toward a Minor Literature*, p. 43.

59   'Kafka ... present[s] the law as a pure and empty form without
     content, the object of which remains unknowable: thus, the law can be
     expressed only through a sentence, and the sentence can be learned
     only through a punishment. No one knows the law's interior. No one
     knows what the law is in the Colony; and the needles of the machine
     write the sentence on the body of the condemned, who doesn't know
     the law, at the same time as they inflict their torture upon him'.
     Deleuze and Guattari, *Kafka: Toward a Minor Literature*, p. 43. Also
     see 'The Penal Colony', in Kafka, *The Transformation and Other
     Stories*, pp. 127–53.

60   Deleuze and Guattari, *Kafka: Toward a Minor Literature*, p. 43.

61   Deleuze and Guattari, *Kafka: Toward a Minor Literature*, pp. 43–4.

62   Key here, for Deleuze and Guattari, is the role played by Max Brod,
     the man who edits and orders the chapters of *The Trial* after Kafka's
     death, who publishes the book against Kafka's expressed interests.
     That is to say, we need to be critically sensitive to 'the ways that Max
     Brod arranged things to support his thesis of negative theology'.
     Deleuze and Guattari, *Kafka: Toward a Minor Literature*, p. 44.

63   Deleuze and Guattari, *Kafka: Toward a Minor Literature*, pp. 43–4.

64   Franz Kafka, *The Trial* (London, 1992), p. 120.

65   Kafka, *The Trial*, p. 120.

66   Kafka, *The Trial*, p. 121.

67   Kafka, *The Trial*, p. 121.

68   Here again we could emphasize the political importance of the ques-
     tion, of being able or capable of posing your own questions, questions
     that always-already carry with them orders and imperatives that shape
     the world and social-political relations. See note 20.

69   Kafka, *The Trial*, p. 121.

70   Kafka, *The Trial*, p. 122.

71   Kafka, *The Trial*, p. 123.

72   Kafka, *The Trial*, pp. 123–4.

73   Kafka, *The Trial*, p. 124.

74   Deleuze and Guattari, *Kafka: Toward a Minor Literature*, p. 45.

75   Kafka, *The Trial*, p. 124.

76   Deleuze and Guattari, *Kafka: Toward a Minor Literature*, p. 56.

77   Kafka, *The Trial*, p. 119.

78   'Justice is desire ... Everyone in fact is a functionary of justice – not
     only the spectators, not only the priest and the painter, but also the
     equivocal young women and the perverse little girls who take up so
     much space in *The Trial*. K's book in the cathedral is not a prayerbook
     but an album of the town; the judge's book contains only obscene
     pictures. The law is written in a porno book. Here, it is no longer a

question of suggesting an eventual falsity of justice but of suggesting its desiring quality'. Deleuze and Guattari, *Kafka: Toward a Minor Literature*, p. 49.

79   Kafka, *The Trial*, p. 119.
80   Kafka, *The Trial*, p. 119.
81   'The best part of Max Brod's book on Kafka is when Brod tells how listeners laughed at the reading of ... *The Trial* "quite immoderately". We don't see any other criteria for genius than the following: the politics that runs through it and the joy that it communicates'. Deleuze and Guattari, *Kafka: Toward a Minor Literature*, pp. 95–6. 'Max Brod recalls that when Kafka gave a reading of *The Trial*, everyone present, including Kafka himself, was overcome by laughter ...'. Gilles Deleuze, *Masochism: Coldness and Cruelty* (New York, 1991), p. 85.

## Painting

1   Gilles Deleuze and Félix Guattari, *A Thousand Plateaus: Capitalism and Schizophrenia* (London, 1988), pp. 167–91.
2   Gilles Deleuze, *Francis Bacon: The Logic of Sensation* (London, 2005).
3   Of course, the existence of such key differences between Levinas and Deleuze-Guattari could be taken to immediately render problematic the kind of cross-comparison I am suggesting here. For example, Peter Hallward rather caustically suggests that Deleuze's philosophy is quite foreign to the 'inane reverence for the other' that one would find in a philosopher such as Levinas. See, Peter Hallward, *Out of This World: Deleuze and the Philosophy of Creation* (London, 2006), p. 159. As I have already said, my guiding intuition here is that a montage or cross-cutting of Levinasian and Deleuze-Guattarian images of the face is a legitimate hermeneutical strategy inasmuch as it helps foreground the idea that Deleuze and Guattari's critical engagement with painting has an ethical as well as political tenor.
4   Emmanuel Levinas, *Totality and Infinity* (Pittsburgh, 1995), pp. 194–5.
5   Jean-Paul Sartre, *Being and Nothingness* (New York, 1956).
6   Laura Mulvey, 'Visual Pleasure and Narrative Cinema', *Screen*, 16, 3, (1975), pp. 6–18.
7   John Berger, *Ways of Seeing* (London, 1972).
8   Levinas, *Totality and Infinity*, p. 195.
9   Simon Critchley, *Infinitely Demanding* (London, 2007), pp. 57–8.
10  In *Infinitely Demanding* Critchley advances his thesis that 'ethical experience' begins with the experience of a demand to which the subject gives approval. So no meaning can be invested in the ethical,

the moral, in 'our' sense of the good – whatever the 'good' may mean here or however it is filled out at the level of content – without this experience of a demand that requires approval. Importantly, this formal structure of ethical experience implies certain claims regarding the structure of subjectivity, it tells us about the nature of the self. Put simply, the self is that thing that shapes itself in relation to the good or, in stronger philosophical terms, the demand of the good founds the self and is the 'fundamental principle of the subject's articulation' as Critchley puts it. However, this notion of 'ethical subjectivity' is 'split', or the subject of 'ethical experience' is a 'split subject' precisely because the 'demand' placed on it cannot, in principle, ever be met by the subject: the demand remains, in Critchley's Levinasian terms, 'heteronomous'. Perhaps predictably, but nonetheless interestingly and skillfully, Critchley develops this Levinasian image of a 'split subject' by connecting his insights to a body of thought to which Levinas was rather suspicious: namely, psychoanalysis. Critchley suggests that the heteronomy that structures 'ethical experience' – the demand of the good which exceeds me and always remains outside of me – can be seen as a 'traumatic' experience, where an experience of trauma is precisely an experience of something that comes from the outside to disrupt the I. From a psychoanalytic perspective, it is important to understand trauma as that which gives rise to neurosis, an experience of traumatic neurosis. What does this mean? Well, as the name suggests, traumatic neurosis is the product of experienced trauma, an experience whose effect continues to plague and live on in the subject, sometimes long after the traumatic event. As with other forms of neurosis it inevitably involves compulsion and repetition, where the original traumatic event is compulsively revisited and repeated by the subject, and the subject itself becomes constituted through the compulsive repetition of the trauma. Coming back to Levinas, Critchley suggests that the 'Levinasian ethical subject is a traumatic neurotic' precisely because the subject's experience of the other is an 'obsessive experience of a responsibility that persecutes me with its sheer weight', where 'I am the other's hostage'. This means, finally then, that if the ethical subject is defined by the approval of a heteronomous and traumatic demand, it is a divided subject, 'constitutively split between itself and a demand it cannot meet'. See, Critchley, *Infinitely Demanding*, pp. 56–63.

11  Critchley, *Infinitely Demanding*, pp. 32–7.

12  Immanuel Kant, 'What is Enlightenment?', in S. Lotringer and L. Hochroth (eds), *The Politics of Truth: Michel Foucault* (New York, 1995), pp. 7–8.

13  Kant, 'What is Enlightenment?', p. 7.

14  'What must be acknowledged is the heteronomous constitution of autonomy, that the ethical demand is refractory to our cognitive powers and the other person can always resist whatever concept under which we may try to subsume him'. Critchley, *Infinitely Demanding*, p. 57.

15  Levinas, *Totality and Infinity*, p. 291.

16  I have written at more length on how Habermas's concept of an intersubjectivity grounded in communicative action informs his ethics and politics. See Robert Porter, *Ideology: Contemporary Social, Political and Cultural Theory* (Cardiff, 2006), chapters two and three in particular. Also, and more recently, see my 'Habermas in Pleasantville: Cinema as Political Critique', *Contemporary Political Theory*, 6, 4 (2007), pp. 405–18.

17  'Because others attribute accountability to me, I gradually make myself into the one who I have become in living together with others. The ego, which seems to me to be given in my self-consciousness as what is purely my own, cannot be maintained by me solely through my own power, as it were for me alone – it does not "belong" to me. Rather, this ego always retains an intersubjective core because the process of individuation from which it emerges runs through the network of linguistically    mediated    interactions'.    Jürgen    Habermas, *Postmetaphysical Thinking* (Cambridge, 1998), p. 170.

18  'This curvature of space expresses the relation between human beings. That the Other is placed higher than me would be a pure and simple error if the welcome I make him consisting in perceiving a nature. Sociology, psychology, physiology are thus deaf to exteriority'. Levinas, *Totality and Infinity*, p. 291.

19  Deleuze and Guattari, *A Thousand Plateaus*, p. 177.

20  Charles Taylor, *Multiculturalism and the Politics of Recognition* (New Jersey, 1992), pp. 72–3.

21  Taylor, *Multiculturalism and the Politics of Recognition*, p. 73.

22  Deleuze and Guattari, *A Thousand Plateaus*, pp. 177–8.

23  On the importance of dialogue to the disruption and reformation of identity, see, among others, Charles Taylor, *The Ethics of Authenticity* (London, 1991), pp. 47–8.

24  Deleuze and Guattari, *A Thousand Plateaus*, p. 178.

25  Deleuze and Guattari, *A Thousand Plateaus*, p. 178.

26  Deleuze and Guattari, *A Thousand Plateaus*, p. 301.

27  In addition to connecting together Levinas and Deleuze-Guattari politically, we may also speculate about certain connections or parallels in the way they think the aesthetic, or, more particularly, the materiality of art. Eric Alliez, for example, points to certain parallels between Levinas's early work – most particularly *Existence and Existents* – and

Deleuze and Guattari's last collaborative work *What is Philosophy?*. Here Alliez sees in both Levinas and Deleuze-Guattari a concern to emphasize the importance of what we can call an aesthetics of sensation, where an 'aesthetics of sensation' implies the notion that art has the material and concrete capacity to take us beyond embodied subjectivity and everyday worldly perception. See Eric Alliez, *The Signature of the World: What is Deleuze and Guattari's Philosophy?* (London, 2006), pp. 72–4.

28   Deleuze often liked to repeat the Guattarian dictum: 'before Being, there is politics'. See, for example, Gilles Deleuze and Claire Parnet, *Dialogues* (London, 1987), p. 17.

29   Gilles Deleuze, *Bergsonism* (New York, 1991).

30   Deleuze and Guattari, *A Thousand Plateaus*, pp. 105–6.

31   It could be argued that painting a picture of Deleuze and Guattari as anarchists all too quickly commits their thought to the norms and conventions of an anarchist politics which in actuality is quite foreign to the ontology that is at the heart of their critique of state-form. For example, Alain Badiou directly counters this idea when through the evocation of the Deleuzian concept of 'crowned anarchy' he importantly stresses the need to think the crown 'above all else'. It is misplaced according to Badiou to think of Deleuze as a radical and egalitarian anarchist opposing state power. For Badiou, 'Deleuze's conception of thought is profoundly aristocratic'. Alain Badiou, *Deleuze* (London, 2000), p. 11.

32   On the idea that Deleuze and Guattari's critique of representation in the state-form embodies a quasi anarchism, see Todd May, *The Political Philosophy of Poststructuralist Anarchism* (Pennsylvania, 1994), p. 85. Also, see Paul Patton, *Deleuze and the Political* (London, 2000), p. 8.

33   Critchley, *Infinitely Demanding*, pp. 122–3.

34   'Anarchy ... cannot be sovereign. It can only disturb, albeit in a radical way, The State, prompting isolated moments of negation *without any* affirmation. The State, then, cannot set itself up as a whole.' Quoted in Critchley, *Infinitely Demanding*, p. 122.

35   Deleuze, *Bergsonism*, p. 15.

36   Keith Ansell-Pearson, for instance, stresses the key importance of Bergson in the development of what he calls a Deleuze-Guattarian 'ethological ethics' and the 'nonhuman becomings of the human' that are expressed or created through it. See Keith Ansell-Pearson, *Germinal Life* (London, 1999), p. 179. We will again have occasion to acknowledge the importance of Bergsonian thought in the next chapter when discussing Deleuze and Guattari's writings on architecture.

37  John Berger, 'Prophet of a Pitiless World', *The Guardian*, 29 May 2004.

38  'It is with God that everything is permitted, not only morally, since acts of violence and infamies always find holy justification, but aesthetically, in a much more important manner, because the divine Figures are wrought by a free creative work, by a fantasy in which everything is permitted ... In Giotto's *Stigmatization of St Francis* (1297–1300) Christ is transformed into a kite in the sky, a veritable airplane, which sends the stigmata to St Francis, while the hatched lines that trace the path to the stigmata are like free marks, which the Saint manipulates as if they were strings of the airplane-kite. Or Tintoretto's *Creation of the Animals* (1550): God is like a referee firing the gun at the start of a handicapped race, in which the birds and fish leave first, while the dog, the rabbits, the cow, and the unicorn await their turn'. Deleuze, *Francis Bacon*, p. 7.

39  Deleuze, *Francis Bacon*, p. 61.

40  Deleuze, *Francis Bacon*, p. 61.

41  Deleuze, *Francis Bacon*, p. 62.

42  For an interesting discussion of this and other ideas that informed the making of *Twin Peaks* see Chris Rodley, *Lynch on Lynch* (London, 1997) pp. 155–90.

43  Deleuze, *Francis Bacon*, p. 65.

44  Deleuze, *Francis Bacon*, pp. 67–8.

45  Deleuze, *Francis Bacon*, p. 66.

46  David Sylvester, *Interviews with Francis Bacon* (London 1993), p. 11. An image of this work can be found at: http://www.artquotes.net/masters/bacon_paintings.htm.

47  'It is like the emergence of another world. For these marks ... are irrational, involuntary, accidental, free, random. They are non-representative, nonillustrative, nonnarrative ... It is here that the painter works with a rag, a stick, brush or sponge: it is here that he throws the paint with his hands. It is as if the hand assumed an independence and began to be guided by other forces, making marks that no longer depend on either our will or our sight. These almost blind manual marks attest to the intrusion of another world into the visual world of figuration ... The painter's hand intervenes in order to shake its own dependence and break up the sovereign optical organization: one can no longer see anything, as if in a catastrophe, a chaos'. Deleuze, *Francis Bacon*, p. 71.

48  Sylvester, *Interviews with Francis Bacon*, p. 90.

49  Deleuze, *Francis Bacon*, p. 67.

50  Sylvester, *Interviews with Francis Bacon*, p. 92.

51  Sylvester, *Interviews with Francis Bacon*, p. 93.

[52] Sylvester, *Interviews with Francis Bacon*, p. 93.

[53] 'You see, I want the paintings to come about so that they look as though the marks had a sort of inevitability about them ... It's one of the reasons I don't really like abstract expressionism. Quite apart from its being abstract, I just don't like the sloppiness of it'. Sylvester, *Interviews with Francis Bacon*, p. 94.

[54] Deleuze, *Francis Bacon*, p. 68.

[55] Deleuze, *Francis Bacon*, p. 68.

[56] James Williams, 'Deleuze on J. M. W. Turner: Catastrophism in Philosophy?' in K. Ansell-Pearson (ed.), *Deleuze and Philosophy* (London 1997), p. 242.

[57] Deleuze, *Francis Bacon*, pp. 70–1.

[58] Bacon's long-standing commitment to portraiture was underlined by a Scottish National Gallery of Modern Art exhibition, *Francis Bacon: Portraits and Heads*, held in 2005. Composed of some fifty four works, and covering almost a sixty-year period of Bacon's life, this exhibition set out to show, in the words of its own tag-line, 'Bacon's singular achievement in defining what portraiture could be'.

[59] 'Francis Bacon's portraits ... tell the story of Bacon's involvement with certain individuals – with lovers such as Peter Lacy and George Dyer; with fellow painters such as Lucian Freud and Frank Auerbach; with drinking companions such as Muriel Belcher, Isabel Rawsthorne and Henrietta Moraes; and with friends such as Bruce Bernard, the photo-historian; John Hewitt ...; and the French writer and philosopher Michel Leiris. They also form a biography of the artist himself, from the early heads painted with dash and verve, to the portraits at the end of his life: faint, spectral, verging on the sentimental ...' Andrea Rose, 'Introduction' to Richard Calvocoressi and Martin Hammer, *Francis Bacon: Portraits and Heads* (Edinburgh, 2005), p. 7.

[60] Deleuze, *Francis Bacon*, p. 15.

[61] Deleuze, *Francis Bacon*, pp. 15–16.

[62] Deleuze, *Francis Bacon*, p. 16. An image of this work can be found at: http://www.artdaily.com/index.asp?int_sec=11&int_new=24248&int_modo=1.

[63] Deleuze, *Francis Bacon*, p. 16. An image of this work can be found at: http://www.artquotes.net/masters/bacon_paintings.htm.

[64] Deleuze, *Francis Bacon*, p. 16. An image of this work can be found at: http://members.tripod.com/~pinkfreudian/at/gdyerdog.html.

[65] The question of how a given body responds to an experience of the 'intolerable' is something that not only preoccupies Deleuze in *Francis Bacon*. It is very much part of his and Guattari's work on Kafka, where Kafka's response is one of humour; 'to laugh', as Thoburn puts it, 'in the midst of the intolerable'. See Nicholas Thoburn, *Deleuze,*

*Marx, Politics* (London, 2003), p. 146. Of course, Kafka's sense of humour, and the political critique mediated through his use of humour, is something we have already discussed in chapter one. Deleuze also detects a similar sense of humour, a similar laughter in the midst of the intolerable, in Foucault, particularly the Foucault of *Discipline and Punish*. Here Deleuze thinks of Foucault's meticulous descriptions of things such as 'anti-masturbation machines for children' as a kind of comic writing and thinking which spark 'fits of laughter', 'unexpected laughter which shame, suffering or death cannot silence'. Foucault's humour implies a 'joy' that wants to 'destroy whatever mutilates life'. See Gilles Deleuze, *Foucault* (Minneapolis, 1988), p. 23.

[66]  Deleuze, *Francis Bacon*, p. 18.
[67]  Deleuze, *Francis Bacon*, p. 17.
[68]  Sylvester, *Interviews with Francis Bacon*, p. 81.
[69]  Deleuze, *Francis Bacon*, p. xii.
[70]  Sylvester, *Interviews with Francis Bacon*, p. 82.


## Architecture

[1]  Deleuze and Guattari, *What is Philosophy?* (London, 1994), p. 186.
[2]  Ronald Bogue, *Deleuze on Music, Painting and the Arts* (London, 2003), p. 163.
[3]  The Foucauldian and Leibnizian motifs or concepts of 'outside', 'light' and 'folding' will be discussed as the chapter develops.
[4]  For instance, in *Anti-Oedipus* Deleuze and Guattari map out a particular concept of the city or town as a connective 'network' determined by its relation to other towns and also, for example, by the 'commercial' forces that give shape to it. For a good treatment and development of this point, see Andrew Ballantyne, *Deleuze and Guattari for Architects* (London, 2007), p. 80. Indeed, the notion that economic forces give shape to the built environment of the town or city is something that we will come back to, particularly in the final part of the chapter.
[5]  Although we will at times speak in general terms about a Deleuze-Guattarian aesthetics or conception of art, the focus in this chapter will obviously tend towards a particular concern for architecture and built form. For a broader conception of Deleuze and Guattari's theory of the arts, see Bogue, *Deleuze on Music, Painting and the Arts*, pp. 163–95.
[6]  Deleuze and Guattari, *What is Philosophy?*, pp. 183–4.
[7]  David Sylvester, *Interviews with Francis Bacon* (London, 1993), p. 93.
[8]  Deleuze and Guattari, *What is Philosophy?*, p. 184.

9    Elizabeth Grosz rightly emphasizes that any given space is 'never fixed or contained', is 'always open to various uses in the future', and that this 'different inhabitation' of space implies a politics or the potential for emergent and different subjectivities: for example, she explicitly mentions the development of 'queer space' as implying the conversion of 'existing spaces' into 'new forms for new functions'. Elizabeth Grosz, *Architecture from the Outside* (London, 2001), p. 8.

10   Deleuze and Guattari, *What is Philosophy?*, pp. 184–5.

11   Gilles Deleuze, *Foucault* (Minneapolis, 1988), pp. 57–8.

12   Deleuze, *Foucault*, pp. 57–8.

13   Deleuze, *Foucault*, p. 58.

14   This stress on stylization is something we find in the fiction of J. G. Ballard (I am particularly thinking here about works from the early to mid 1970s such as *High Rise* and *Crash*, the latter interestingly was published the very same year as Foucault's *Discipline and Punish*), where 'stylization' implies the body's encounter with an impersonal form/technology/architecture and is then shaped and reshaped through this encounter.

15   Deleuze, *Foucault*, p. 79.

16   Deleuze, *Foucault*, pp. 96–7.

17   Gilles Deleuze, *Bergsonism* (New York, 1991).

18   Alain Badiou, *Deleuze* (London, 2000), p. 43. For a helpful and well-informed treatment of the concept of the virtual see also, among others, James Williams, *Gilles Deleuze's Difference and Repetition* (Edinburgh, 2003); Peter Hallward, *Out of This World: Deleuze and the Philosophy of Creation* (London, 2006).

19   Deleuze, *Bergsonism*, p. 105.

20   Deleuze, *Bergsonism*, p. 97.

21   Deleuze, *Bergsonism*, p. 98.

22   Deleuze, *Bergsonism*, p. 98.

23   Brian Massumi, 'Sensing the Virtual, Building the Insensible', *Architectural Design*, 68, 6, (1998), p. 20.

24   Massumi, 'Sensing the Virtual, Building the Insensible', p. 21.

25   Gilles Deleuze, *Negotiations* (New York, 1995), p. 158.

26   Deleuze and Guattari, *What is Philosophy?*, pp. 100–1.

27   See, most obviously, Greg Lynn (ed.), *Folding in Architecture* (West Sussex, 2004).

28   For a good critical discussion and contextualization of Lynn's place in shaping architectural theory in accordance with Deleuze-Guattarian concerns, see Paul Harris, 'To See With the Mind and Think Through the Eye', in I. Buchanan and G. Lambert (eds) *Deleuze and Space* (Edinburgh, 2006), pp. 36–60.

29   Greg Lynn, *Folds, Bodies and Blobs* (Brussels, 1998), pp. 111–12.

30 'By virtual definition', Massumi argues, 'the built form does not resemble ... the virtual forces generating it'. Massumi, 'Sensing the Virtual, Building the Insensible', p. 21.

31 Lynn, *Folds, Bodies and Blobs*, p. 53.

32 Lynn, *Folds, Bodies and Blobs*, p. 54.

33 Lynn, *Folds, Bodies and Blobs*, p. 54.

34 It is worth noting with James Williams the limits of continually seeking to analyse the architectural significance of Deleuze and Guattari's thought by locking it into some 'already vague and unproductive modern-postmodern debate'. That is to say, we would do well to take Williams's advice and caution slightly against a tendency in the architectural theory and practice of, say, Peter Eisenman (or indeed Greg Lynn) which sometimes seeks to place and play Deleuze or a concept of Deleuze-Guattarian architecture against vague notions of the 'modern' and 'postmodern'. See, J. Williams, 'Deleuze's Ontology and Creativity: Becoming in Architecture', *Pli*, 9, (2000), p. 206.

35 Lynn, *Folds, Bodies and Blobs*, pp. 55–6.

36 John Rajchman, *Constructions* (Massachusetts, 1998). Also, see John Rajchman, *The Deleuze Connections* (Massachusetts, 2000).

37 Gilles Deleuze and Claire Parnet, *Dialogues* (London, 1987), p. vii.

38 Deleuze and Parnet, *Dialogues*, p. vii.

39 Gilles Deleuze, *Empiricism and Subjectivity: An Essay on Hume's Theory of Human Nature* (New York, 1991), p. 101.

40 Deleuze and Parnet, *Dialogues*, p. 57.

41 Rajchman, *Constructions*, p. 115.

42 Rajchman, *Constructions*, p. 109.

43 Rajchman, *Constructions*, p. 56.

44 This is a point taken up in a slightly different way by Massumi when he writes that 'the problem with the dominant modes in cultural and literary theory is not that they are too abstract to grasp the concreteness of the real. The problem is that they are not *abstract enough* to grasp the real [or] ... the concrete'. See Brian Massumi, *Parables for the Virtual* (London, 2002), p. 5.

45 Rajchman, *Constructions*, p. 57.

46 Rajchman, *Constructions*, p. 66.

47 Rajchman, *Constructions*, pp. 64–5.

48 Deleuze and Guattari, *A Thousand Plateaus*, p. 510.

49 Of course, this very foreshortened, even caricatured, image of Plato's *Republic* is an illustrative gesture, rather than a developed critique, or it is a rather uncomplicated critique of the supposed lack of complication to be found in the Platonic Form. The irony of this is not lost on Rajchman and he later qualifies his remarks regarding Plato suggesting

that a more complicated abstraction of the 'and' is also immanent to other aspects of Platonic thought. See Rajchman, *Constructions*, p. 66.

50    Deleuze and Guattari, *A Thousand Plateaus*, p. 510.

51    Rajchman, *Constructions*, p. 66.

52    For a more general or broader analysis of the political geography of contemporary Belfast, see Peter Shirlow and Brendan Murtagh, *Belfast; Segregation, Violence and the City* (London, 2006).

53    The language of a 'post-conflict' Belfast or Northern Ireland is not exclusive to a well meaning, but thoroughly uncritical, journalism that abstracts from and masks the continuing reality of ethno-sectarian antagonism and violence. It is also, importantly, the language used by urban planners and property developers who see their interests being served in this new 'post-conflict' dispensation. See Shirlow and Murtagh, *Belfast*, p. 2.

54    At the time of writing, Northern Ireland has a functioning Assembly and Executive in which all the main parties share power.

55    For a useful historical overview of the building of the westlink, and an analysis of some of the political opposition to its construction, see, M. Cinalli, 'Socio-Politically Polarized Contexts, Urban Mobilization and the Environmental Movement: A Comparative Study of Two Campaigns of Protest in Northern Ireland', *International Journal of Urban and Regional Research*, 27, 1, (2003), pp. 158–77.

56    I am grateful to my friend Daniel Jewesbury for reminding me of this.

57    Indeed, we could even go so far as to say that some media coverage in Northern Ireland functions as a form of 'propaganda' for 'peace'. On this point, see Steve Baker and Greg McLaughlin, 'Housetraining the Paramilitaries: The Media and the Propaganda of Peace in Northern Ireland', in C. Coulter and M. Murray (eds) *Northern Ireland After the Troubles?: A Society in Transition* (Manchester, 2008), pp. 253–271.

58    'Belfast is far from being the post-conflictual city that is dreamed of by planners [and] investors …'. Shirlow and Murtagh, *Belfast*, p. 2. For an extended analysis of the persistent and deep rooted nature of this sectarian segregation, see Shirlow and Murtagh, *Belfast*; for example, chapters one, three and four.

59    One of the most striking examples of this kind of narrative folding occurred when the Swedish company IKEA opened a huge store in Belfast in December 2007. The coverage of the store's opening was very much anchored in the political notion that inward investment by such a huge global player was clear evidence to suggest Northern Ireland's transition to a 'post-conflict' dispensation. Indeed, one of the most illuminating images to emerge from this coverage was that of the then first and deputy first ministers of the Northern Ireland Executive

(that is, Ian Paisley and Martin McGuinness) sitting happily smiling on an IKEA sofa together. And, clearly by design, on the wall behind Paisley and McGuinness (these erstwhile Unionist and Republican antagonists) the tag-line or motto of the company prominently reads: 'home is the most important place in the world'.

60    For details of this reconstruction and development of the westlink, see http://www.wesleyjohnston.com/roads/a12westlinkupgradedetails.html.

61    I say initially because, at the time of writing, Carpenter's proposed sculpture has now been put on hold by Belfast City Council; primarily, it seems, for economic reasons.

62    Accessed from the BBC Northern Ireland News website, 2 April 2008; http://news.bbc.co.uk/1/hi/northern_ireland/4329710.stm.

63    In this way, we could say that cynicism is reactionary, or ideologically regressive, to the extent that it ends with a shrug of the shoulders and never really interrogates the political conditions that give rise to it. For a fascinating and insightful analysis of the way this kind of cynicism ends in such quietism, see Slavoj Žižek, *The Sublime Object of Ideology* (London, 1989).

64    Deleuze and Guattari, *What is Philosophy?*, p. 100.

65    Deleuze and Guattari, *What is Philosophy?*, p. 99.

66    For example, during the late 1970s it became increasingly difficult for my elder brother to keep going to school as it was located 'over there' towards the Falls Road end of Broadway. Finally, as sectarian tension heightened and as the built environment started to concretize this sectarian segregation through the building of the westlink, our parents decided to place him in another school.

67    Deleuze and Guattari, *What is Philosophy?*, p. 164.

68    What I am about to say here has been importantly influenced by conversations I have had with Daniel Jewesbury. That is to say, my brief speculations as to what might constitute a kind of dematerialized monument to the social-political forces at play in and around Broadway follow clearly and directly from Daniel. Indeed, Daniel, and a fellow artist Jem Finer, put forward a proposal for such a work to the Belfast City Council when it initially canvassed for ideas in 2005.

69    This is but an example, and obviously I would not want to imply that my experiences are in some way privileged.

70    On the idea that the interpretation and evaluation of forces is always a critical-political question, see Gilles Deleuze, *Nietzsche and Philosophy* (London, 1986), p. 91. This is a point that I develop at greater length in my Ph.D. thesis. See Robert Porter, *Deleuze, Geophilosophy, Criticism* (unpublished Ph.D. thesis, Queens University, Belfast, 1999), pp. 13–40.

## Conclusion

1   Gilles Deleuze and Félix Guattari, *A Thousand Plateaus: Capitalism and Schizophrenia* (London, 1988), p. 89.

2   I have made this point elsewhere in the context of arguing for a notion of cinema as a form of 'political critique'. See my 'Habermas in Pleasantville: Cinema as Political Critique', *Contemporary Political Theory*, 6, 4 (2007), pp. 405–18.

3   Deleuze and Guattari, *A Thousand Plateaus*, p. 4.

4   'We have been criticized for overquoting literary authors. But when one writes, the only question is which other machine the literary machine can be plugged into, must be plugged into. Kleist and a mad war machine, Kafka and a most extraordinary bureaucratic machine … Literature is an assemblage'. Deleuze and Guattari, *A Thousand Plateaus*, p. 4.

5   Peter Hallward, *Out of This World: Deleuze and the Philosophy of Creation* (London, 2006), p. 162.

6   'The politics of the future are likely to depend less on virtual mobility than on more resilient forms of commitment, on more integrated forms of coordination, on more resistant forms of defence'. Hallward, *Out of This World*, p. 162.

7   Of course, one of the key intuitions that I would take from Deleuze and Guattari here is that any normative prescriptions that we assume to guide political action are always-already (that is immanently) caught up in the bodies or forms of subjectivity in and through which they are given expression. In other words, normative prescriptions do not and cannot condition political action and subjectivity precisely because political actions are shaped by forms of the 'good' (with their attending normative prescriptions) that emerge in and through the production of subjectivity as such. For further discussion of this point – and an analysis of how this more 'Spinozian' conception of the 'good' differentiates Deleuze and Guattari from, say, the 'Kantianism' of thinkers such as Habermas and Žižek – see my *Ideology: Contemporary Social, Political and Cultural Theory* (Cardiff, 2006), pp. 122–31.

8   Although at one point Hallward does seem to make a slight concession to the work of Jean-Jacques Lecercle and the latter's stress on the importance of the 'slogan' in Deleuze's conception of language and political practice. Hallward, *Out of This World*, p. 185.

9   My point, then, is a simple one: I have engaged in a particular *use* of Deleuze and Guattari, a *use* that is not indifferent to the world and the values pulsing through it, but a use that has as Guattari would say 'ethico-political implications', implying as it does 'responsibility' to the

'thing' that is 'created' by this *use*. Importantly, Guattari refers to the assumption of this kind of 'responsibility ... to the thing created' as a gesture that is not only 'ethico-political' but also 'ethico-aesthetic'. That is to say, he insists on the importance of what I want to call an *aestheticization of political thinking*. See Félix Guattari, *Chaosmosis: An Ethico-Aesthetic Paradigm* (Sydney, 2006).

# Bibliography

Alliez, E., *The Signature of the World: What is Deleuze and Guattari's Philosophy?* (London, 2006).

Ansell-Pearson, K., *Germinal Life* (London, 1999).

Badiou, A., *Deleuze* (London, 2000).

Baker, S. and McLaughlin, G., 'Housetraining the Paramilitaries: The Media and the Propaganda of Peace in Northern Ireland', in C. Coulter and M. Murray (eds) *Northern Ireland After the Troubles?: A Society in Transition* (Manchester, 2008), pp. 253–271.

Ballard, J. G., *Crash* (London, 1973).

Ballard, J. G., *High Rise* (London, 1975).

Ballantyne, A., *Deleuze and Guattari for Architects* (London, 2007).

Berger, J., *Ways of Seeing* (London, 1972).

Berger, J., 'Prophet of a Pitiless World', *The Guardian*, 29 May 2004.

Bogue, R., *Deleuze on Cinema* (New York, 2003).

Bogue, R., *Deleuze on Literature*, (New York, 2003).

Bogue, R., *Deleuze on Music, Painting and the Arts* (New York, 2003).

Cinalli, M., 'Socio-Politically Polarized Contexts, Urban Mobilization and the Environmental Movement: A Comparative Study of Two Campaigns of Protest in Northern Ireland', *International Journal of Urban and Regional Research*, 27, 1, (2003), 158–77.

Critchley, S., *On Humour* (London, 2002).

Critchley, S., *Infinitely Demanding* (London, 2007).

Calvocoressi, R. and Hammer, M., *Francis Bacon: Portraits and Heads* (Edinburgh, 2005).

Deleuze, G., *Nietzsche and Philosophy* (London, 1986).

Deleuze, G., *Foucault* (Minneapolis, 1988).

Deleuze, G., *Spinoza: Practical Philosophy* (San Francisco, 1988).

Deleuze, G., *Bergsonism* (New York, 1991).

Deleuze, G., *Empiricism and Subjectivity: An Essay on Hume's Theory of Human Nature* (New York, 1991).

Deleuze, G., *Masochism: Coldness and Cruelty* (New York, 1991).

Deleuze, G., *Expressionism in Philosophy: Spinoza* (New York, 1992).

Deleuze, G., *The Fold: Leibniz and the Baroque* (London, 1993).

Deleuze, G., *Difference and Repetition* (London, 1994).

Deleuze, G., *Negotiations* (New York, 1995).

Deleuze, G., *Francis Bacon: The Logic of Sensation* (London, 2005).

Deleuze, G. and Guattari, F., *Anti-Oedipus: Capitalism and Schizophrenia* (London, 1984).

Deleuze, G. and Guattari, F., *Kafka: Toward a Minor Literature* (Minneapolis, 1986).

Deleuze, G. and Guattari, F., *A Thousand Plateaus: Capitalism and Schizophrenia* (London, 1988).

Deleuze, G. and Guattari, F., *What is Philosophy?* (London, 1994).

Deleuze, G. and Parnet, C., *Dialogues* (London, 1987).

Grosz, E., *Architecture from the Outside* (London, 2001).

Guattari, F., *Chaosmosis: An Ethico-Aesthetic Paradigm* (Sydney, 2006).

Habermas, J., *Moral Consciousness and Communicative Action* (Cambridge, 1990).

Habermas, J., *Postmetaphysical Thinking* (Cambridge, 1998).

Hallward, P., *Out of This World: Deleuze and the Philosophy of Creation* (London, 2006).

Harris, P., 'To See with the Mind and Think Through the Eye', in I. Buchanan and G. Lambert (eds) *Deleuze and Space* (Edinburgh, 2006), pp. 36–60.

Hobbes, T., *Leviathan*, (London, 1968).

Hyman, R., *A Biography of Kafka* (London, 1981).

Kafka, F., *The Transformation and Other Stories* (London, 1992).

Kafka, F., *The Trial* (London, 1992).

Kant, I., 'What is Enlightenment?', in S. Lotringer and L. Hochroth (eds), *The Politics of Truth: Michel Foucault* (New York, 1995), pp. 7–20.

Lecercle, J. J., *The Violence of Language* (London, 1990).

Lecercle, J. J., *Deleuze and Language* (Basingstoke, 2002).

Levinas, E., *Totality and Infinity* (Pittsburgh, 1995).

Lynn, *Folds, Bodies and Blobs* (Brussels, 1998).

Lynn, G. (ed)., *Folding in Architecture* (West Sussex, 2004).

Mackenzie, I., *The Idea of Pure Critique* (London, 2004).

Massumi, B., *A User's Guide to Capitalism and Schizophrenia: Deviations from Deleuze and Guattari* (London, 1993).

Massumi, B., 'Sensing the Virtual, Building the Insensible', *Architectural Design*, 68, 6, (1998), 16–24.

Massumi, B., *Parables for the Virtual* (London, 2002).

May, T., *The Political Philosophy of Poststructuralist Anarchism* (Pennsylvania, 1994).

Mulvey, L., 'Visual Pleasure and Narrative Cinema', *Screen*, 16, 3, (1975), 6–18.

Olkowski, D., *Gilles Deleuze and the Ruin of Representation* (Berkeley, 1999).

Patton, P., *Deleuze and the Political* (London, 2000).

Plato, *The Republic* (London, 1975).

Porter, R., *Deleuze, Geophilosophy, Criticism* (unpublished Ph.D. thesis, Queens University, Belfast, 1999).

Porter, R., *Ideology: Contemporary, Social, Political and Cultural Theory* (Cardiff, 2006).

Porter, R., 'Habermas in Pleasantville: Cinema as Political Critique', *Contemporary Political Theory*, 6, 4 (2007), 405–18.

Porter, R. and Porter, K. A., 'Habermas and the Pragmatics of Communication: a Deleuze-Guattarian Critique', *Social Semiotics*, 13, 2 (2003), 129–45.

Rajchman, J., *Constructions* (Massachusetts, 1998).

Rajchman, J., *The Deleuze Connections* (Massachusetts, 2000).

Robertson, R., *Kafka* (Oxford, 2004).

Rodley, C., *Lynch on Lynch* (London, 1997).

Sartre, J. P., *Being and Nothingness* (New York, 1956).

Shapiro, M. J., *Deforming American Political Thought* (Lexington, 2006).

Shirlow P. and Murtagh, B., *Belfast; Segregation, Violence and the City* (London, 2006).

Simons, J., 'Ideology, Imagology, and Critical Thought: The Impoverishment of Politics', *Journal of Political Ideologies*, 5, 1, (2000), 81–103.

Sylvester, D., *Interviews with Francis Bacon* (London 1993).

Taylor, C., *The Ethics of Authenticity* (London, 1991).

Taylor, C., *Multiculturalism and the Politics of Recognition* (New Jersey, 1992).

Thoburn, N., *Deleuze, Marx, Politics* (London, 2003).

Williams, J., 'Deleuze on J. M. W. Turner: Catastrophism in Philosophy?', in K. Ansell-Pearson (ed.), *Deleuze and Philosophy* (London 1997), pp. 233–46.

Williams, J., 'Deleuze's Ontology and Creativity: Becoming in Architecture', *Pli*, 9, (2000), 200–19.

Williams, J., *Gilles Deleuze's Difference and Repetition* (Edinburgh, 2003).

Žižek, S., *The Sublime Object of Ideology* (London, 1989).

# Index